ROBBIE

The unofficial and unauthorised biography of
ROBBIE WILLIAMS
by Karen Anderson

Published by
Kandour Ltd
1-3 Colebrook Place
London N1 8HZ

This edition printed in 2004 for
Bookmart Limited
Registered Number 2372865
Trading as Bookmart Ltd
Blaby Road
Wigston
Leicester LE18 4SE

First published June 2004

ISBN 1–904756–13–1

Production services:
Metro Media Ltd

Author: Karen Anderson

With thanks to: Jenny Ross, Emma Hayley,
Lee Coventry, Paula Field

Cover design: Mike Lomax
Cover Image: Rex Features

Inside Images: Rex Features

© Kandour Ltd

Printed and bound by Nørhaven Paperback, Denmark

ROBBIE WILLIAMS

FOREWORD

This series of biographies is a celebration of celebrity. It features some of the world's greatest modern-day icons including movie stars, soap personalities, pop idols, comedians and sporting heroes. Each biography examines their struggles, their family background, their rise to stardom and in some cases their struggle to stay there. The books aim to shed some light on what makes a star. Why do some people succeed when others fail?

Written in a light-hearted and lively way, and coupled with the most up-to-date details on the world's favourite heroes and heroines, this series is an entertaining read for anyone interested in the world of celebrity. Discover all about their career highlights – what was the defining moment to propel them into superstardom? No story about fame is without its ups and downs. We reveal the emotional rollercoaster ride that many of these stars have been on to stay at the top. Read all about your most adored personalities in these riveting books.

ROBBIE WILLIAMS

CONTENTS

Fact file 8

Introduction 11

The early years 19

Take That 31

Guided by angels 47

Take This 59

Singing and swinging .75

Escape and Escapology 87

Live floor show 103

Mr Entertainment 115

Giving something back 133

Ladies, feuds and fallouts 147

The future 163

Discography 170

Awards . . . . :.174

Other books in the series 177

ROBBIE WILLIAMS

FACT FILE

Born: 13 February 1974
Place: North Staffordshire Royal Infirmary, Newcastle-Under-Lyme, Staffordshire
Height: 6' 1"
Eyes: Green
Hair: Dark brown

Mother: Theresa Jeanette (Jan) Williams – publican, shop owner, florist and counsellor

Father: Peter Williams (stage name Pete Conway) comedian and singer

Sister: Sally, nine years older than her brother, she started the Robbie Williams fan club which she ran before having her first child, in 2000

School: Mill Hill Primary School, Tunstall and St Margaret Ward RC High School, Tunstall

Favourite football team: Port Vale

Star sign: Aquarius

ROBBIE WILLIAMS

FACT FILE

Chinese Horoscope: Tiger

Possessing a magnetic personality and great charm, Tigers are born leaders and very ambitious. They have a natural, raw appeal and great charisma which other signs find very attractive. Tigers are very sensitive and prone to mood swings and emotional outbursts.

Career high:

(1) Release of his most famous single, *Angels*, in December 1997 gave his failing solo career the jump-start it needed and saw Williams gain respect within the music industry. It led to his memorable Glastonbury Festival appearance in front of a record 100,000+ crowd in June 1998.

(2) Summer 2003 – Weekends of Mass Distraction European Tour hit the road and Williams played sell out gigs in 25 stadiums in 20 countries – the highlight of which was his three consecutive gigs at Knebworth Park in August to a record 375,000 fans. The resulting DVD *What We Did Last Summer – Robbie Williams Live at Knebworth*, is the fastest selling music DVD ever in the UK and the album, *Live At Knebworth* sold an amazing 117,863 copies in its first week, and has sold over a million to date.

1

Introduction

ROBBIE WILLIAMS

INTRODUCTION

Professionally, things can't get much better for Robbie Williams. In 2002 he signed the largest record deal in UK history (and the second largest in the world) when he re-signed with EMI for an estimated £80 million. The following year he performed to over 1.5 million fans on his European stadium tour. The resulting DVD from the UK-leg was made into *What We Did Last Summer – Robbie Williams Live at Knebworth 2003* and became the fastest selling music DVD of all time, after he'd broken all attendance records at Knebworth with three consecutive sell-out gigs.

ROBBIE WILLIAMS

INTRODUCTION

Since going solo Robbie Williams has achieved five number one hit singles, five number one hit albums; 10 Brits and 3 Ivor Novello awards.

When he left the highly successful boy band Take That in 1995 his future seemed far from rosy. He got off to a shaky start – he was unable to record any solo material because of existing contractual obligations; he released four consecutive singles that all failed to hit the top spot and was recovering from excessive partying when he should have been promoting his early solo material. His nemesis, Gary Barlow, had already recorded two number one singles and the press had virtually written Williams off. But then in December 1997, he released his Christmas single, *Angels*.

Angels re-launched his career – it remained in the Top 10 for 11 weeks and sold an amazing 820,000 copies – even though it only reached number four in the charts. It has become a favourite with young and old – played at weddings and funerals alike – a song that has been very good to its singer. Such was its success that Williams could have stuck with melancholic ballads for the rest of his career and done very nicely, but instead he has gone from strength to

ROBBIE WILLIAMS

INTRODUCTION

strength by mixing his musical styles and influences until it has become difficult to place him into any one genre. He definitely sings pop, but there's also a lot of rock and soul, and a bit of disco in there, with the occasional rap thrown in for good measure. His lyrics can be funny and poignant, acutely raw and painful or downright arrogant and cocksure – and he's never scared to force a rhyme. His lyrics are unusually personal, he's had his problems, his knock-backs and his love stories – it's all there in his songs, laid bare. In 2001 he confounded everyone when he released an album of swing hits, a tribute to the songs that made Frank Sinatra, Dean Martin and Sammy Davis Jr household names in the Fifties – nobody saw it coming and it was an amazing triumph – Robbie Williams the crooner was a success.

Just listening to Williams' records, however, only gives you access to half of his talent – true he has a powerful and distinctive voice, and sings clever and witty lyrics, but he is a natural showman and was born to perform. When Williams is live on stage he raises the roof, belting out massive rock anthems and slow ballads with the same intense power, he holds his audience's attention in the palm of his hand and

INTRODUCTION

never disappoints. His live videos are a testament to his performing talent and his promotional videos are works of art.

This book tells the story of Williams' journey to the top – stopping off on the way to take a look at his songs, his videos, his shows, his relationships, his rows, his record deals and his troubled soul.

2

The early years

ROBBIE WILLIAMS

THE EARLY YEARS

Robbie Williams was brought up in the Staffordshire city of Stoke-on-Trent and led a typical working class life until he was 15. He was born on 13 February 1974 in the North Staffordshire Royal Infirmary, Newcastle-Under-Lyme to parents Jan and Pete, and nine year-old sister Sally. He initially lived in the Tunstall area of the city until his parents took over The Red Lion pub in Burslem in 1975. His parents had been together for seven years (Sally is Jan Williams' daughter from a previous marriage) and had married in 1970, but the domestic bliss of them all living together under one roof was to end before

ROBBIE WILLIAMS

THE EARLY YEARS

Williams was three, when his father left. His mother brought him up, but he sill had contact with his father.

Williams' father was a comedian and local entertainer who was (and still is) known by his stage name Pete Conway. Originally a policeman, he took up touring the club circuit with his stand-up comedy act in the late sixties and turned professional in the early seventies soon after he married Jan. He was regularly away from home touring the country and was a finalist (having won his own individual heat) in the television talent show *New Faces* in 1974 (he came third behind Les Dennis) shortly before Williams was born. While his itinerant lifestyle suited him well, it wasn't ideal for family life and he was persuaded by his wife to settle down and take over The Red Lion pub. The pub was close to Port Vale FC's football ground and as he is a life-long supporter (as is Williams) it was in the perfect location.

Since his son became famous Conway has been interviewed many times and asked why he left the family home in 1977. Although many interviews have suggested some tension between Williams' parents, the overriding reason was that

THE EARLY YEARS

he enjoyed the freedom of being on the road and settling down just wasn't for him. This lack of responsibility may have had a lasting, detrimental effect upon Williams – it is difficult to tell as Williams himself has given different answers when questioned about it. He has been famously quoted as saying it had no effect on him as he had a happy childhood with his mum, sister and grandparents – yet much has been made of Williams' lyrics in *My Culture*, the record he made with One Giant Leap in 2002.

In a now familiar talk/rap, he expresses his feelings towards his father, singing about tears and years of loneliness.

After a few years of running the pub on her own Jan Williams gave it up and became a florist in Tunstall, where the family returned to live. Williams attended the Mill Hill Primary School and nursed a slow-burning wish to be an entertainer, which was to blossom into a burning ambition to become an actor. As an out-going, funny child he was always up for telling jokes, doing impressions and belting out a tune or two. As a toddler he entertained the punters in his parent's pub, entered himself into a talent contest while on holiday in Spain with his family – he

ROBBIE WILLIAMS

THE EARLY YEARS

sang *Summer Nights* from *Grease* – and while in Torremolinos aged four, his mother found him busking to fellow holiday-makers.

After he appeared in a primary school production of *Oliver*, his mother recognised some natural talent and ambition and helped him channel his energy into amateur dramatics. During his time at St Margaret Ward RC High School he appeared in many local productions including *Chitty Chitty Bang Bang* with the Stoke Charity Pantomime and Drama Company and in *Hans Christian Andersen*, *Pickwick* and *Oliver* again. At the ages of 14, he aptly played a cheeky Artful Dodger for the North Staffordshire Amateur Operatic & Dramatic Society. He also had a walk-on part in the Channel 4 soap opera, *Brookside*.

As his experience treading the boards fuelled his desire to become an actor, so too did his nights watching his father perform. As an extension of his work on the comedy circuit of pubs and clubs, especially in the Midlands and the north, Pete Conway had residencies in holiday hotels or at holiday camps. He worked as a compere, with hotel residencies – usually in the summer – where he would host an evening's entertainment and intersperse it with his own jokes and renditions of

THE EARLY YEARS

many club standards including Frank Sinatra and Dean Martin covers. When he didn't have a hotel residency he worked the holiday camp circuit, often performing at one Butlins or Pontins site for the whole summer season. He was a successful entertainer and as a teenager Williams would often visit his father on location, frequently staying with him for a fortnight or more during the height of the summer season. Williams found his father's lifestyle very attractive and admired him for it. He would watch him work an audience, admire his showmanship and professionalism and take a bit of the glamour home with him and tell his school friends all about it.

Williams was kept grounded during his childhood by his close relationship with his mother and sister – and his grandparents. Effectively a single parent, Jan Williams had to work hard to support her family and instilled many important values in her children, one of which was the importance of family. Many singer/songwriters write personal lyrics, but these are usually about love won or lost. Williams is unlike many of his contemporaries in that a lot of his lyrics are about his family or dedicated to them. He *wrote One of God's Better People* (it appears on his first album,

THE EARLY YEARS

Life Thru a Lens) for his mum and although they are bound to appear on a Mother's Day card soon the lyrics are simple and poignant, describing his mother as a very special person. When asked by *Top of the Pops* magazine how his mum reacted to the song, he bashfully replied: "She cried. It meant a lot to her." Miles away from this sentimentality are the lyrics in his hit single *Come Undone* (April 2003). In this song he painfully sings about his past problems and how ashamed he is of his behaviour and the hurt he has caused his mother, calling himself "scum".

It is clear that this veiled apology is for his mum (not his dad) because it betrays an intimacy of their shared life together.

Still wearing his heart on his sleeve, he wrote *Phoenix From The Flames* (appears on his second album, *I've Been Expecting You*) for his sister Sally. Sally worked for the Take That fan club and set up the Robbie Williams Fan Club when her brother went solo. She ran the fan club until she had her first son Freddy in 2000 and in 2001 Williams dedicated his BRIT award to his new nephew. He *wrote Nan's Song* (appears on *Escapology*) as a tribute to his paternal grandmother, Bertha (Betty) Williams

THE EARLY YEARS

after she died in 1998. His maternal grandfather, Jack Farrell, was also a great influence in his formative years and he is honoured not in song, but permanently on his skin, by the tattoos on his wrist.

Although there was an element of show business in his early life – both from his dad and his own acting experience – it was on a minor scale and was very grass roots in its nature. There is a great tradition of working class comedy in the Midlands. Stoke-on-Trent was an established port of call on the comedy circuit in the seventies.

His acting was also on a local scale and nothing in his early life gave an indication of the star he would become. Indeed, he hadn't been in the least bit academic at school, being content to act out his chosen role as the class clown. So when he became a double glazing salesman after leaving school and only lasted three months in the job, his future was completely uncertain.

However, his mother's chance sighting of an advert in *The Sun* newspaper, from a new band looking for a fifth member was to change everything – the band was called Kick It, soon to be changed to Take That, taken from the slogan Take That and Party from a Madonna poster. Jan

ROBBIE WILLIAMS

THE EARLY YEARS

Williams encouraged her son to apply, even though it was in contrast to his acting ambitions, and quickly compiled an impressive CV for him. He auditioned and four weeks later found out he had landed the job that was going to change his life – as the fifth member of Take That – on the same day he discovered he'd failed all his exams.

3

Take That

ROBBIE WILLIAMS

TAKE·THAT

ake That had already formed as a four-piece group when 15-year-old Robbie Williams joined. The band consisted of Gary Barlow, Mark Owen, Jason Orange and Howard Donald – four young hopefuls from Manchester, managed by Nigel Martin-Smith and looking for a record deal. They had all given up their day (and night) jobs – a club singer, a tea boy and bank clerk, a painter and decorator and a mechanic respectively – and were paid a retainer while rehearsing for their big break.

Gary Barlow was already a gifted songwriter when he first met Take That's future manager

TAKE THAT

Nigel Martin-Smith. At 15, he entered a BBC Pebble Mill songwriting competition called a Song for Christmas and was a short-listed finalist with his entry *Let's Pray For Christmas*. Although he didn't win the competition he made a lot of contacts and was touting a demo tape of songs around the industry looking for a manager when he met up with producer, Nigel Martin-Smith. A self-made millionaire, Martin-Smith had made his money by setting up a successful modelling and casting agency in the eighties. With a keen interest in pop music, he was impressed with the meteoric rise to fame of the US teen sensation New Kids on the Block and believed he could put together a similar ensemble in Britain – combining new and catchy pop tunes, a group of good looking boys and some funky dance steps.

Martin-Smith recognised Barlow's vocal and song writing talent early on. He had already written two of Take That's future hits – *A Million Love Songs and Why Can't I Wake Up With You* – by the time he was 16. But Barlow was not an archetypal front man – he just didn't look like a pop star and admitted to Martin-Smith that he was uncomfortable dancing. He needed some other cute bandmembers. (Ironically, when Barlow did

TAKE THAT

eventually go solo he changed his image and became very svelte, rugged and moody – the black and white photographs on his first solo album attest to this – the perfect front man). Barlow was already friends with Mark Owen and had formed a group with him a couple of years earlier called The Cutest Rush, when Owen was only 14. Fortunately, Owen could sing and was a good dancer, but most of all and not to disparage any of his other talents, he was great looking – a massive plus for a young, female fan base. Added to this mix were two of Manchester's best breakdancers Jason Orange and Howard Donald who had set up Street Beat and toured the country participating in urban dance competitions. Orange was also a regular dancer on Granada TV's late night music show *The Hit Man and Her*. They were a little older than the others and looked as if they had lived a little, a plus for the older female fan in her 20s. In addition, both were amazingly good-looking, fit, toned and athletic (Donald famously demonstrated his athleticism by wrapping his legs around his neck during Take That's first appearance on BBC1's *Live and Kicking*). In hindsight it is obvious that Martin-Smith was on to a winner with this combination, especially

TAKE THAT

when he added cheeky, jack-the-lad Williams, who came loaded with buckets full of attitude and charm, to the mix. The pop scene was not yet used to the phenomena of the manufactured boy band, so Take That was new and fresh and welcomed with open arms by young teenage girls.

But they were not an overnight success. It took a lot of hard graft to break the charts. Originally targeting the gay market, they cut their first teeth as a five-piece group touring the North's gay clubs, with their high-energy dance tunes. Their leather-clad, six-packed bodies – especially Orange and Donald – performing complicated dance routines were a great attraction.

Their first single, *Do What U Like*, was released on Martin-Smith's own Dance UK label in July 1991, to mixed reviews. The most memorable thing about the single wasn't the song (it only reached number 82 in the UK charts), but its camp, homoerotic video, which featured all five of them with their bottoms on show, covered in jelly. And although the boys are clearly larking about in the video, suggesting that it was all a bit tongue-in-cheek, it certainly got the band talked about and was enough to interest RCA, who

TAKE THAT

signed them up in September 1991.

In November they released their next single, *Promises*, which reached number 38 in the charts, followed by *Once You've Tasted Love* in February 1992, which reached number 47. As they were signed up so quickly to RCA the band thought that they would have a hit single a lot earlier than they did and found it demoralising to never peak higher than the middle of the chart. Barlow infamously remarked that Take That were rapidly becoming "the most famous group in Britain for not having a hit".

But all that was about to change with the release in June 1992 of *It Only Takes a Minute*, their upbeat take on the Tavares hit, to great fanfare. Although the success of a cover version may have been a minor blow to Barlow's ego initially as he had penned their other singles, it didn't matter because it reached number 7 in the charts and Take That had broken into the world of pop stardom. Every teen magazine and kid's TV programme wanted a piece of the action – and the boys were happy to give it. Within weeks their cheeky grins and semi-naked bodies were posted up on bedroom walls country-wide.

But the much-coveted number one spot in

TAKE THAT

the charts was to elude them for yet another year. Their first album, *Take That and Party* (released in August 1992), peaked at number two in the UK album charts. This was an amazing feat considering that their first seven singles actually appear on it – bearing witness to the fact that their increasingly dedicated fans were prepared to spend all their pocket money on them. The remaining four releases from the first album all did well – *I Found Heaven*, the first Take That single to feature Williams sharing lead vocals (Number 15), *A Million Love Songs* (Number 7*)*, *Could It Be Magic* (Number 3), *Why Can't I Wake Up With You* (Number 2). To clarify their popularity with Britain's teenagers Take That picked up a Best Single BRIT for *Could It Be Magic* and received seven awards at the *Smash Hits* Poll Winners Party that year.

Take That's blend of high energy disco tunes and slow melodic ballads, with the odd cover version thrown in, was a great success and 1993 was their year. They had three consecutive number one single hits, the first with *Pray* (July), *Relight My Fire* (featuring Lulu in September) and *Babe* (December) the first single to feature Mark Owen on lead vocals, unfortunately it

TAKE THAT

missed the much coveted 'Christmas number one' spot when it was knocked off by Mr Blobby. The icing on the cake for the boys that year was the release of their second album, *Everything Changes*, which smashed into the album chart at number one on 23 October.

Once they had reached the top no other pop band could touch them. Throughout 1994 and 1995 they were still recording hit after hit even though other boy bands like East 17 and Boyzone were there to offer stiff competition, not to mention the emergence of credible Britpop bands like Oasis, Blur and Pulp who were filling up the charts. Every single they released hit the top spot, with the exception of *Love Ain't Here Anymore* which only reached number three in June 1994 and when they toured their tickets sold out minutes after they went on sale. Their third album, *Nobody Else*, went straight in at number one in the album chart in May 1995. Number one singles for *Everything Changes*, *Sure*, *Back For Good*, *Never Forget* and *How Deep Is Your Love* brought the band's grand total to eight – making them one of the bestselling bands of all time.

While many serious music critics derided Take That's offerings as chart fodder, there were a

TAKE THAT

few signs that they won them over towards the end. When *Back For Good* was released in March 1995, it was hailed as the best single they had ever released winning over their harshest critics who thought their sound had matured and showed a lot more substance and integrity than their earlier hits. It even broke the US Top 10, a market they had never really cracked (*Back For Good* was the only Take That single to make the Billboard Top 10, where it remained for 13 weeks – it first charted on 12 August 1995).

Although the band's commercial success went from strength to strength, there were rumours as early as 1994 that all was not well within the band itself. Williams has claimed since the band broke up that he was never really happy when he was in Take That, but other members of the band claim that this is simply untrue and they had loads of great times together, suggesting that their acrimonious breakup marred any happy memories. He was certainly close friends with Mark Owen. But by 1994 Williams had started to drink heavily and experiment with drugs and was becoming increasingly bored and embarrassed with the band's polished dance routines and their clean-cut good boys of pop

TAKE THAT

image. He had run-ins with Martin-Smith because he'd fluff his dance steps, he was always tired and hungover, he appeared on TV when he was told not to, and in general had stopped towing the party line. Added to this was Williams' frustration at playing second fiddle to Gary Barlow, who was seen as the only songwriting talent in the band. It would only be a matter of time before he would upset the apple cart for good – and the stardom they shared as Take That would indeed become someone else's dream.

What ever happened to:

Gary Barlow (born 20 January 1971, Frodsham, Cheshire) had two number one solo hits after Take That's break up with *Forever Love* and *Love Won't Wait* and a number one album with *Open Road*. Since then we have heard little of him and he was last seen on ITV's popular drama, *Heartbeat* and he has continued to write songs for others, including Atomic Kitten. He is now married with two young children. In March 2004, *Heat* magazine asked top television presenters Ant and Dec who they would most like to see on their hit show, *I'm A Celebrity, Get Me Out Of*

TAKE THAT

Here. They revealed that they would love to have Gary Barlow on and it is believed that he has been invited to appear on the 2005 show.

Mark Owen (born 27 January 1974, Oldham, Greater Manchester) launched a solo career and had two hits in the top five with *Child* and *Clementine*, but after disappointing sales of his first album, *The Green Man*, he was dropped by RCA. Having spent many years out of the public eye, with the exception of a TV programme on celebrity scooters, Owen was a contestant and the eventual winner of Channel 4's *Celebrity Big Brother* in 2002 and the exposure has done him no harm at all. He came across as a very ordinary, calm and very relaxed person – incredibly likeable and still very cute. Since then, Owen appeared as one of Williams' special guests at Knebworth 2003 and they sang the Take That classic, *Back for Good*, for old time's sake. He then went on to release his second solo album, *In Your Own Time* (MCA) in November of the same year. This aptly named album came seven years after his first solo outing with *The Green Man*, and is strikingly different in that Owen wrote all 13 tracks on the album, including the two single releases *Four*

ROBBIE WILLIAMS

TAKE THAT

Minute Warning (August) and *Alone Without You* (October).

Jason Orange (born 10 July 1970, Manchester) – little has been heard of Orange since the split. In 1998, *The Sun* reported that he had gone travelling for a year and had spent a lot of time in the Caribbean. Since then he has turned to acting and has appeared in the Lynda La Plante's drama, *Killer Net* – about an addictive computer game that enables the player to carry out the perfect murder. Orange played DJ, Brent Moyer. He also appears in the 2002 film *Lullaby of Clubland*, starring Orlando Bloom.

Howard Donald (born 28 April 1968, Droylsden, Manchester) – not much has been seen or heard from the once dread-locked dancer of the group. He is now a well-respected club DJ in Manchester and regularly performs in Europe, most recently with gigs in Germany, Spain, Italy, Belgium and Holland. He had some song writing success when he penned the 1997 hit *Crazy Chance* for Kavana. In the 8 August 1999 issue of *OK! Magazine* he appeared in an 11-page spread with his partner Vicky, and their young daughter Grace.

TAKE THAT

Take That Discography

ALBUMS

Take That and Party (August 1992)
Highest chart position: 2
Everything Changes (October 1993)
Highest chart position: 1
Nobody Else (May 1995)
Highest chart position: 1
Greatest Hits (May 1996)
Highest chart position: 1

SINGLES

Do What U Like (July 1991)
Highest chart position: 82
Promises (November 1991)
Highest chart position: 38
Once You've Tasted Love (January 1992)
Highest chart position: 47
It Only Takes a Minute (May 1992)
Highest chart position: 7
I Found Heaven (August 1992)
Highest chart position: 15

TAKE THAT

A Million Love Songs (September 1992)
Highest chart position: 7
Could It Be Magic (December 1992)
Highest chart position: 3
Why Can't I Wake Up With You (February 1993)
Highest chart position: 2
Pray (July 1993)
Highest chart position: 1
Relight My Fire (September 1993)
Highest chart position: 1
Babe (December 1993)
Highest chart position: 1
Everything Changes (March 1994)
Highest chart position: 1
Love Ain't Here Anymore (June 1994)
Highest chart position: 3
Sure (October 1994)
Highest chart position: 1
Back For Good (March 1995)
Highest chart position: 1
Never Forget (July 1995)
Highest chart position: 1
How Deep Is Your Love (March 1996)
Highest chart position: 1

4

Guided by angels

ROBBIE WILLIAMS

GUIDED BY ANGELS

Williams' increasingly bad behaviour and complete disassociation with the 'clean living' rules that Take That had agreed to abide by, had forced the band's management team, led by Nigel Martin-Smith, into a corner. His high profile jaunt to Glastonbury in June 1995, where he appeared in unscheduled interviews, frolicked on stage with Oasis, and enjoyed himself with Britpop stars, proved to be the last straw.

When he returned to band rehearsals after Glastonbury, it was made very clear that his management team and fellow band members were furious with him. There still remains some

GUIDED BY ANGELS

conjecture as to whether Williams was asked directly to leave or in a fit of pique said he was off. However his position within the band had become untenable and as a result of the ensuing row, Williams left the rehearsal room and the band forever. The news of Williams' departure made every front page and was even reported on ITV's *News at Ten*.

Although Williams may have appeared not to care about the rest of the band and his future with it at the time, his subsequent downfall over the following months was, in part, a result of his unplanned exit from the band. He had told the other members he wanted to leave and they were quietly preparing for it, but he did not realise that his departure would come about as quickly as it did. Mark Owen told *BBC Radio 1* at the time that the boys had an agreement with each other that they would give six months' notice if any of them wanted to leave. As a result of this, Williams may have thought he had a couple of months grace to decide about his immediate future, but instead was forced to cope with life without Take That in full public view and without any plans.

Williams has stated in many interviews, at

the time and since, that life in Take That was very restrictive and controlled, and to put many of his comments mildly, he was not encouraged to think for himself. The pressure of now having to cope on his own coupled with the complete freedom to do so caused much of his extreme behaviour at the time. When asked why he was miserable at the time of the split, Williams commented: "I didn't like the band I was in. I didn't like what I was famous for. I didn't like what fame had brought me. I felt as though I was talentless. I felt as though I was the butt of every joke, and every joke about me was right."

At only 21, Williams' self-esteem was incredibly low considering his success, fame and wealth – but being famous for being in a boy-band was not what he wanted. He wanted credibility, and having famous friends like Liam and Noel Gallagher wouldn't have the longevity he was after. He was going to have to wait a couple of years before he became respected for his ability as a singer, songwriter and performer – so for the time being, infamy would have to suffice.

Apart from successful stints guest presenting the likes of Channel 4's morning show, *The Big Breakfast* and BBC1's *Top of the Pops* and *Going*

GUIDED BY ANGELS

Live, Williams' engagement diary was pretty empty of gigs, so he filled the void with wild partying. He gained three stone in weight, looked bloated and older than his years, and was seen at every showbiz party on the circuit usually worse for wear. He may have started his partying days at George Michael's house in St Tropez among other A-list celebrities but once he was on a roll he turned up everywhere.

However, while Williams was out having a good time, some of his habits were causing great concern to those closest to him. Eventually, in October 1996, he agreed to get help and was initially counselled by Beechy Colclough (who had treated other celebrities in the past) and in June 1997 checked himself into Clouds, a private clinic in Wiltshire. He stayed there for six weeks, got better, lost weight and was able to start work again. In a *Top of the Pops* interview in September 1997 he explained what had happened to him and how he had recovered. He described that he had finally come to terms with who he was, learnt to accept himself and to stop punishing himself. He ended the interview saying how proud he was of what he had achieved.

While Williams was struggling with his

personal demons he was also fighting, with the help of his new manager Tim Abbott, a lengthy legal battle with Nigel Martin-Smith and RCA/BMG records over Williams' right to pursue his solo career. There was a clause in his contract that prohibited Williams from leaving RCA when he left Take That and he spent six months trying to extricate himself from the deal. He didn't want to remain with RCA because they were connected to Take That and RCA refused to release him from his contract. Due to appear in court on 26 February 1996 amid rumours that his court case was not strong enough, Williams and RCA came to a last minute out-of-court settlement, with Williams paying an estimated £300,000 (estimates range from £250,000–400,000) in costs and issuing an apology to the record company. A statement issued by Williams noted that he accepted the legality of his contract and remained with BMG (parent company of RCA).

Remaining with RCA/BMG was not what Williams wanted, but as his contract was binding he had little choice but to accept it and move on. However, salt was then rubbed into his wounds when Take That announced on 13 February 1996 that they were splitting up and that Gary Barlow

GUIDED BY ANGELS

and Mark Owen would remain with the label to pursue their solo careers. With three ex-Take That members on the same label, Williams remained unhappy, as he believed his work would be sidelined while Gary Barlow, the proven songsmith of the group, was promoted.

Luckily this wrangle was short lived. Williams signed a £1.5 million contract with Chrysalis/EMI in June 1996, with EMI agreeing to pay RCA £800,000 to release Williams from his contract. Williams released his first single, George Michael's *Freedom*, shortly afterwards on 29 July, a year after he parted company with Take That.

Declaring his break from Take That and his record label simultaneously, *Freedom* was an obvious if somewhat unchallenging choice as his first solo single and left many of his critics unimpressed and sceptical about his future. It did reach number two in the UK charts, but his next releases *Old Before I Die*, *Lazy Days and South of the Border* (all from his first album, *Life Thru a Lens*) had limited success, as did his initial album sales.

Then in December 1997 Williams released *Angels* – and he has never looked back.

GUIDED BY ANGELS

Did Robbie jump or was he pushed?

There was much conjecture over whether Williams quit the band or was asked to leave the group in July 1995, which became the subject of a long legal battle between Williams and Martin-Smith over the next four years. Martin-Smith claimed Williams had left the band, while Williams maintained that he had been forced out.

In a court case in November 1997, Martin-Smith claimed he was owed commission by Williams under the terms of a management agreement signed in 1990. In return, Williams claimed that Martin-Smith had been in breach of his management agreement [claiming that Martin-Smith had encouraged the other members of the band to issue him with an ultimatum over his future with them] and was therefore not entitled to commission. Justice Ferris ruled against Williams and ordered him to pay Martin-Smith £90,000 in unpaid commission as well as a share of his Take That royalties until 2006. The judge found that during a meeting between Williams, Barlow and Orange on 8 July 1995, Williams had been offered two options − to stay with the band for six months and be highly committed for that period, or to leave immediately. He found that Williams chose the latter option. Williams appealed against this ruling and his appeal was held before Justices Beldam, Roch and Mummery in March 1999. They upheld Justice Ferris' earlier ruling and it is believed that the initial £90,000 sum was greatly increased when additional VAT, interest and additional on-going commission was added to it, with unofficial estimates bringing the total bill to approximately £1 million.

5

Take this

TAKE THIS

Angels is a song that has been good to Robbie Williams and no matter what he goes on to achieve in his musical career he will always be expected to sing it when he performs live – or rather his audience will want to sing it with him when he performs live. As soon as the first bars of the intro are played at any Robbie Williams gig the crowd goes wild, and they scramble for the lighters that even non-smokers have brought along for this very song, and hold them aloft as they belt out every word. On paper that sounds corny, cheesy, naff... in reality it is contagious. The combination of the uplifting and melancholy lyrics, combined

TAKE THIS

with Williams' heart-wrenching delivery and the knowledge that he probably has had a bit of luck guiding him through the years make for a powerful and overwhelming experience. But it doesn't stop there, try listening to *Angels* on the car radio and it is difficult to stop yourself singing along. In an article in *Vogue* in October 2000, the writer Justine Picardie tells a funny tale of the comedian David Baddiel's 40th birthday party when he declared *Angels* to be one of the finest songs ever written. Most of his guests immediately joined in the chorus of the song – they knew every word. It has become part of the British psyche and it isn't one of the most popular songs played at funerals for nothing – it has a lasting, emotive appeal.

So much so that it is a surprise to learn that *Angels* only ever reached number four in the UK singles charts. It did, however, hang around the Top 10 for 11 weeks, selling 820,000 copies overall and revived the falling sales of Williams' first album *Life Thru a Lens*, taking it back up the album charts. He had only sold 33,000 copies of the album initially, but this was increased to 300,000 after *Angels* was released, and was enough to take his first album to the number one spot after it had already been in the charts for 28 weeks. It also

TAKE THIS

made people sit up and listen to Williams singing. Since he had gone solo the previous year almost all of the media coverage he had received had been concerned with his life style or his competitive battle with ex-Take That band member, Gary Barlow. Barlow had released his own solo material at the same time and had already had two consecutive number one hits. Williams fuelled this fire when he admitted in a *Vox* magazine interview in October 1997 that he had bought Barlow's album *Open Road* and took it back to the shop the next day, demanding a refund. They did patch up their differences, in public anyway, when both Williams and Barlow appeared on stage together in December 1997 for the Princess Diana Concert for the Hope benefit gig in Battersea Park, London where they, poignantly, sang The Beatle's classic, *Let It Be*. Williams also dedicated *Angels* to Princess Diana that day, winning over any fans he hadn't yet converted.

If Williams was going to have any longevity as a pop star he had to impress his public with the songs he was writing and the CDs he was releasing, rather than with his antics and his Take That notoriety. To this end he parted company with his manager Tim Abbott in October 1996 (see page 73)

TAKE THIS

and joined forces with Tim Clark and David
Enthoven and their company IE Music, in
December 1996. Having worked in the music
business since the Sixties – Clark with Island
Records where he signed up Bob Marley and
Enthoven promoting Roxy Music (then Bryan
Ferry) and T Rex among others – they set up IE
Music in 1991, managing Massive Attack among
other new bands. This deal was an astute move by
Williams as both Clark and Enthoven were well-
respected, very grounded and had extensive
experience in promoting and managing big stars.
They also realised that although Williams' lyrics
were very strong he needed a musician to help him
produce good songs – and to that end they
introduced him to Guy Chambers.

Chambers was 10 years older than
Williams and a seasoned musician when they
first met up in January 1997. He was classically
trained having graduated from the Guildhall
School of Music with a degree in composition in
1984 and an MA and Composition Prize in 1985.
He was relatively unknown when he first
started collaborating with Williams – although he
had been part of The Waterboys and joined World
Party in 1986, set up his own band The Lemon

TAKE THIS

Trees in 1992 and collaborated with songwriter Cathy Dennis and singer Bryan Adams.

Although uncertain of Williams initially (he too was only familiar with his tabloid image) the pair hit it off immediately and famously started work together almost as soon. Which is just as well as Williams has since admitted in numerous interviews that his bravado at having written loads of songs after he had left Take That and was waiting to launch his solo career was beginning to cause him some concern, as he said: "Last year I went around saying 'writing songs is easy'. I made out I had loads of songs and I hadn't... By the beginning of the year I was getting worried about what I was going to do."

Although he didn't have loads of songs waiting to be produced, he did have lots of lyrics and once he started working with Chambers, who added the musical composition, everything gelled together. If Williams had learnt one thing from his days with Take That it was that once you wrote your own songs – as Gary Barlow did – you got taken seriously, and you got royalties. Within days of working together Williams and Chambers had written half of the tracks on *Life Thru a Lens* and both of them knew they had a good thing going. Chambers co-wrote nine tracks on the album and co-produced it with Steve Power. But it wasn't until the success of *Angels* that they knew they would also be commercially successful. The first three releases from the album *Old Before I Die* (released in April 1997, reached number two in the charts); *Lazy Days* (released in July 1997, reached number eight) and *South of the Border* (released in September 1997, reached number fourteen) did relatively well, but with each release the chart position was lower than anticipated and lower than the single before it, with the number one spot becoming ever more elusive. However, each release did mark a progressive move away from his Take That sound and image, especially the Oasis-pastiche, *South of the Border*. Many music critics believe that this early material failed to do as well as his later singles because Williams himself was not around to promote it. He was in rehabilitation during this period – taking counselling from Beechy Colclough from October 1996 and in Clouds rehabilitation clinic from June 1997 for six weeks – and his young ex-Take That fans needed to see their idol on show. This was to change with his first UK solo tour with 14 gigs in October 1997 –

TAKE THIS

and it is no coincidence that by the time *Angels* was released in December 1997 Williams was looking great. He was slim again, had cropped dark hair and was suited and booted in his video – and back on the scene to promote his record. Williams was to obtain a much broader and older fan base as his career progressed, but it had to be nurtured.

His appearance at the BRIT awards in February 1998 was to help with that. He was nominated for two awards Best Single (for *Old Before I Die*) and Best Solo Artist for his work in 1997 but as his contribution that year didn't peak until December with *Angels* it was no surprise when he didn't pick up an award. The BRITs is unique in its attempts to bring together unlikely bedfellows and have them perform a duet. Williams and Tom Jones performing their Full Monty medley set a precedent that many acts have tried to follow since, with only Kylie and Justin Timberlake coming close. (The infamous Madonna/Britney/Christina kiss didn't take place at the BRITs but at the 2003 MTV Awards – the furore this caused matched the publicity both Williams and Jones received for their duet.) Williams and Tom Jones performing together

TAKE THIS

eclipsed the whole evening. Clad in black leather, with eyeliner to match, Williams the showman was at his best, gyrating and crooning at the same time and nearly upstaging Tom Jones into the bargain. *Rolling Stone* magazine was so impressed with the performance that it enthused about Williams' future: "Appearing alongside a singer of Jones' magnitude and talent has given Robbie the credibility to advance his career as a professional rock musician and talented all-round performer."

It certainly did him no harm and could well have gone some way to converting some of his older fans, likewise Tom Jones may have added some younger fans to his huge fan base that night, as sales of his album *Reload* have soared. Their live duet appeared as a bonus track on Williams' next single release *Let Me Entertain You* (March 1998) which reached number three in the charts. Its upbeat, up-tempo cockiness gave us the first glimpse of Robbie Williams the superstar – and helped coin his nickname in the press, Mr Entertainment.

With his appearance at Glastonbury in June 1998 Williams was to exorcise many of his personal demons. The last time he had been on stage at Glastonbury had been with Oasis in 1995 and was

TAKE THIS

the catalyst in his break up from Take That. This time round he gave one of the best performances of his life in front of a 100,000-strong crowd (his biggest audience since Take That's arena tours, and Glastonbury's biggest ever crowd) – not to mention a huge European audience via satellite. He told *MTV* shortly afterwards how scared he was of going on stage. Because it was a respected music festival with respected musicians and a knowledge-able audience, Williams felt that as he was only from a boy band and didn't have the right musical credentials, that people might hate him.

But his rapturous welcome – from young and old alike – when he opened his set with *Let Me Entertain You* put Williams on cloud nine and he didn't come down for quite a while.

Williams the solo performer had finally arrived, 1998 was his year and was to prove to be the pinnacle of his career. His next single, *Millennium* (released in September 1998, it went straight in at the top of the charts) was to give Williams his first ever solo number one and take him into another league. He was now polished, professional and proud of it. *Millennium* uses a string sample from John Barry's celebrated James Bond theme tune from *You Only Live*

TAKE THIS

Twice (the video also features Williams as 007) which is connected to a hip hop beat, making it an infectious and instant hit.

His second album, the ironically named *I've Been Expecting You* gives another nod to the James Bond theme and was released on 28 October and went straight in at number one in the album chart, and helped Williams become the biggest selling album artist of 1998. The album featured his next single release, *No Regrets*, which was written about his break up with Take That. It only reached number four in the charts but was a real favourite with the music critics, especially as it featured backing vocals from Neil Tennant (Pet Shop Boys) and Neil Hannon (Divine Comedy), with many claiming it was one of his finest songs to date.

Williams could do no wrong, two more releases from the album – *Strong*, the self-deprecating ballad was released in March 1999 and peaked at number four. *She's The One/It's Only Us* (written by Chambers' old band mate in World Party, Karl Wallinger) gave Williams his second number one hit in November 1999, and was accompanied by a stylised and very funny video featuring Williams as a championship ice-

TAKE THIS

skater. Other songs of note on the album *are Karma Killer* (reportedly about Nigel Martin-Smith) and *Jesus in a Camper Van*, which courted some controversy in 2000. A High Court Judge in London ruled that Williams and Chambers had substantially copied the song from one written by folk legend, Woody Guthrie entitled *New York Town*. This followed a lawsuit issued by US-based Ludlow Music Inc who had publishing rights to Guthrie's back catalogue of songs and coincidentally, those of Loudon Wainwright III. Wainwright III had adapted Guthrie's original song into his 1971 hit *I Am The Way (New York Town)* with Guthrie's permission, and although Williams and Chambers had credited Wainwright III in the credits to *Jesus in a Camper Van* on both *I've Been Expecting You* and his US-released album *The Ego Has Landed*, they did not credit Woody Guthrie. Williams and EMI had to pay damages, the sum of which was withheld at the time (but estimates put the figure at around £50,000).

As a result of his success in 1998 Williams was nominated for a record-breaking six BRIT awards, and won three for Best Single (*Angels*), Best Video (*Millennium*) and Best Male Artist.

TAKE THIS

He also won two Ivor Novello Awards with Guy Chambers for Most Performed Song (*Angels*) and Songwriter of the Year and he won Best Male at the MTV Europe Awards. The PRS Awards recognised *Angels* as Best Single and Williams/ Chambers won the coveted Songwriter of the Year Award. *The Face* magazine named him 1998 Man of the Year. In addition, Guy Chambers and Steve Power received an IMF Award for Best Producer for *I've Been Expecting You*. The awards for this album and its singles didn't stop in 1998 – *She's The One* won a BRIT Award for Best Single for 1999 and *Strong* won an Ivor Novello Award for Best Song.

ROBBIE WILLIAMS

Goodbye manager number three

Since his split with Take That, Robbie Williams had been in court to disengage himself from a contract with Nigel Martin-Smith, had a dispute with his second manager Kevin Kinsella and in October 1996 parted company with his third manager in a year, Tim Abbott. Abbott and his company Proper Management who had been credited with helping to negotiate his £1 million deal with EMI, was sacked by Williams shortly after the deal was signed. Williams sited his need for artistic freedom as a reason they parted company and simply said it was time to 'move on' in an official statement. Abbott was more vocal and in his statement expressed his profound disappointment that after having worked so hard to turn Williams' career around, the singer should decide to end their relationship.

Over the next two years both parties were tied up in legal wrangling and it is believed that Williams agreed an out of court settlement in late 1998 – the details of which have not been disclosed.

6

Singing and swinging

ROBBIE WILLIAMS

SINGING AND SWINGING

R obbie Williams has an undoubted talent – an ability to write poignant, timeless ballads and roaring stadium shakers – all delivered with the assured confidence and pizzazz of the consummate professional. His celebrated success in 1998 and 1999 – when he literally became known as Mr Entertainment – was a tough act to follow, but it was a challenge he was up to meeting. His third album *Sing When You're Winning* stormed into the charts at number one upon its release in August 2000, followed closely on the heels of the first single release from the album, *Rock DJ* – released in August 2000, it gave Williams his third

SINGING AND SWINGING

number one singles hit.

Although not the best track from the album, *Rock DJ* certainly has the most attitude – it is loud, raucous, party-stomping and in-your-face. Unlike many of Williams' previous hits it doesn't have any hidden personal meaning in its lyrics and it layers a lot of influences into one song. Williams notes in the sleeve notes to *Sing When You're Winning* his personal nod to one of his favourite performers and lyricists Ian Dury, who inspired the rhythm.

Rolling Stone magazine's Barry Walters was one of the first music journalists to notice and applaud the "Barry White violins over a Frankie Goes to Hollywood throb" within the composition. However, the promotional video that accompanied the single was what really got the song noticed. In it, Williams trying to attract the attention of an attractive and aloof female DJ, does the ultimate striptease. First he takes off his clothes, then his skin and throws all that remains of him to the crowd around him.

The video caused a lot of controversy at the time of its release and very cleverly took Williams out of the teen and even the pre-teen market he had been endeavouring to escape for so long. Because it could not be aired on the very kids early

SINGING AND SWINGING

morning television programmes that had in the past helped create his fan base, it allowed Williams to reinvent himself once more.

Sing When You're Winning was praised by music critics and the public alike, and having sold an impressive one million plus copies in the first year of its release, it went quadruple platinum. Celebrating his love of football, the album cover shows Williams being carried aloft in a football kit, by lots of other footballers, who on closer inspection are all Robbie too. The title too is taken from the infamous football chant "you only sing when you're winning" which can be heard on the terraces most Saturday afternoons by a winning team's fans, when taunting the silence of the opposition when they are a goal or two down. And with Williams' love of irony, it is surely also a taunt to anyone that ever doubted his ability.

If you hadn't listened to the whole album before the release of its second single, *Kids*, you'd be mistaken into thinking that *Sing When You're Winning* is much more dance-oriented than Williams' previous efforts. *Rock DJ* and *Kids* are the fastest and most funky from the album, with the remaining tracks sticking with what Williams and Chambers do best – memorable ballads and catchy pop tunes. In *Kids*, Williams famously duets with pop's princess Kylie Minogue and there is clearly a lot of flirtatious chemistry between them. When the single was released in October 2000 Kylie's career had just been successfully relaunched and she had been signed to Parlophone, another subsidiary of EMI (Williams' label Chrysalis is also an EMI subsidiary) – so it made sense for them to work together. *Kids* reached number two in the charts and classically demonstrated how Williams' lyrics can successfully fuse his self-deprecating humour with his now legendary egotism and bravado.

Only Williams could write lyrics advocating his uniqueness and how, on his own, he has helped to raise the economy, adding for good measure that there is no way his record company would let him go now.

Williams released two more singles from the *Sing When You're Winning*, *Supreme* in December 2000 (reached number four) *and Let Love Be Your Energy* in April 2001 (reached number eleven). An unfulfilled quest for love is the subject matter for Williams' favourite track on the album – *Supreme*. It has a definite feel of Gloria Gaynor's massive hit *I Will Survive* in it

SINGING AND SWINGING

and when questioned about this in an MTV interview in the US, Williams jokingly replied that the song was nothing like *I Will Survive* and that everybody who thought so must be wrong.

Without doubt, the best track on the album is *Better Man* – and although a firm favourite when Williams performs it live, he missed out on having his sequel to *Angels* by not releasing it as a single. Maybe that was his point, by saving this gem for the album he would assure continued sales. In September 2001 Williams explained to Adrian Deevoy in *Amica* magazine how he wrote the song. He explained how he had called on John Lennon to send him something. Acknowledging that it might seem arrogant or crazy, he then began to play some chords, which became the verse of the song. Williams went on to say that the song was finished in one hour and that the song is him being honest.

Eternity/Road to Mandalay was released in July 2001 and gave Williams his fourth number one hit single. The former track on this double A-sided single is the only one of Williams' hits not to appear on an album (*Road to Mandalay* appears on `Sing When You're Winning`). A fantastic summer single, it combines all of Williams' trademark

SINGING AND SWINGING

rhyming lyricism with wistful longing.

In a lot of the promotional interviews Williams conducted after the release of *Sing When You're Winning* the interviewers remarked upon Williams state of health. The rumours about Williams' battle with his vices were exacerbated in a punch-up in Stockholm with record producer, Nellee Hooper when attending the MTV Europe Awards in November 2000. Claiming exhaustion and the flu, and being pushed just a bit too far, Williams explained to *BBC Radio 1's* entertainment reporter Briggy Smale why he got into the fight: "Basically, what happened was, he gave me a friendly punch, that I thought was a bit too hard. So I hit him. But honestly, I don't think anyone should ever come to blows, contrary to the stance I've taken on how I think I'm hard just recently..." When Williams later passed out at the event, the tabloids had a field day. Straight after the event, Williams left for a rest and recuperation holiday in Barbados with Guy Chambers. When he returned home to the UK and rehearsals started for his 2001 Sermon on the Mount Tour, Williams declared to his crew and band that the tour would be completely dry – and everyone would have to fall in line with these demands.

SINGING AND SWINGING

Thinking they'd got his number, Williams confounded all his critics by refusing to be pigeon-holed with his next album release *Swing When You're Winning*, released in November 2001. It too went to number one in the album chart and enabled Williams to have a one-off showcase, with full orchestral backing, at the Royal Albert Hall. Earlier that year Williams recorded Sinatra's hit *Have You Met Miss Jones* for the soundtrack of the hit film *Bridget Jones' Diary*. With this under his belt and his love of everything swing – he had grown up listening and singing along to his dad's Frank Sinatra, Dean Martin and Sammy Davis Jr records and while on tour with him for their book *Somebody Someday*, the journalist Mark McCrum testified to the fact that he kissed their photos (along with that of Mohammed Ali) for luck every night before he went on stage – it seemed the right thing to do. It was also the least expected thing for him to do, which must have been some of the attraction.

There was, however, a lot to sort out because Williams didn't just want to go into the studio and record this classic material from the Fifities and Sixties – he wanted to do it properly. This meant recording it at Capitol Studios in LA where the original Rat Pack set had recorded their material,

SINGING AND SWINGING

with many of the musicians that had actually played with Sinatra, Martin and Davis. To record the album Williams worked with some of the world's legendary jazz greats including Harold Jones, the drummer with the Count Basie Orchestra, the tenor saxophone legend Pete Christlieb, trumpeting maestro, Chuck Findley, and Sinatra's pianist for over 30 years, Frank Miller. The legendary sound engineer Al Schmitt, who had also worked with Sinatra, produced the album – altogether it had a very strong pedigree. Williams admitted to being incredibly nervous and humbled because he was able to work with so many jazz legends and famously thanked every single musician personally for agreeing to play with him before he sang a single note in the studio.

Williams also included some first rate celebrity collaborations on the album – these included duets with Jane Horrocks, Rupert Everett, his best friend Jonathan Wilkes and of course, Nicole Kidman. Their cover of the Frank and Nancy Sinatra's 1967 hit *Somethin' Stupid* was number one in December 2001 – Williams' first Christmas number one. On completion of the album, a jubilant Williams told the press that he had more fun making the album than

SINGING AND SWINGING

ever before. He did have one complaint though – that his fingers had become sore from too much clicking. He diagnosed this complaint as 'swing finger'.

The album was promoted with a one-off gig at the Albert Hall on 10 October 2001,which was recorded and later broadcast by the BBC.

Aptly, 2000 and 2001 were both very good years for Williams commercially and if many thought recording a swing album of classic hits was a rash decision and that Williams had pushed himself just a bit too far in what he could achieve, they were definitely mistaken – he had pulled off a blinder. He also added a lot more awards for his trophy cabinet. He won Best Song for *Rock DJ* at the European Music Awards; BRIT Awards for Best Single (*Rock DJ*), Best Video (*Rock DJ*) and Best Male Solo Artist; he won Best Special Effects in a Video for *Rock DJ* at the MTV Video Music Awards and at the Capital Radio Awards he won Best Album *for Sing When You're Winning*. For good measure he was *GQ* magazine's Solo Artist of the Year 2001.

7

Escape and Escapology

ROBBIE WILLIAMS

ESCAPE AND ESCAPOLOGY

I n December 2001 Williams moved to Los Angeles. It was initially seen as a temporary bolt-hole – away from the spotlight in England – so that he could take a year off and have time to chill out and recuperate after the gruelling schedule he'd put himself through since 1998. It was now time to have a well-earned rest. Whether he was going there to crack America – the only market that had so far eluded him – was open to speculation. Williams himself cleared up the rumours when he explained the following year that he was still living there because it gave him some anonymity and

ESCAPE AND ESCAPOLOGY

took him out of the spotlight and its continual scrutiny. In November 2002 he said: "For about six years I have known that for me to establish any kind of life without being under the microscope I'd have to leave England and I haven't wanted to, and it made me cry..."

Williams' enjoyment of the US and the fact that he can walk down the street unmolested has lasted, he still lives there and enjoys the escapism it affords. It also agrees with him physically – almost gone are the torrid tales of drunken abandon that used to hog the tabloid headlines and in their place are reports of a more composed, sober and mature pop star.

Despite good intentions, that planned year off didn't actually happen – Williams and Chambers kept on working whether they intended to or not is unclear, but it seems as if they were compelled to keep on writing – with time on their hands it was the obvious distraction. While in Barbados in 2001 they had started working on some new material that they would develop and expand in LA. There are many reports that during this period Williams and Chambers were not getting on as famously as they had in the past, mainly because Williams wanted to change direction musically.

ESCAPE AND ESCAPOLOGY

Williams explained that he had begun to hate Robbie Williams and that it was time to reinvent himself again. He believed that he could only do it without Chambers as they had become too closely interlinked with each other.

Two years earlier when releasing his third album, *Sing When You're Winning*, Williams had dedicated it to Chambers declaring, "He's as much Robbie as I am" – so maybe that was now the problem. While working on the new material that would make up Williams' fifth album, *Escapology*, the pair sorted out their differences and created a critically acclaimed masterpiece. Williams became seriously involved with its production and promotion for the first time, and he even designed the new 'RW' logo (allegedly on the back of a cigarette box) for all his newly branded material. Williams wanted to present his record label with the total package, the finished product that he had complete control in creating. But Williams didn't have a record label anymore. His contract with EMI had expired in the summer of 2002.

When word got out to the press that Williams had a new album ready to hit the shelves a furore broke out. On 10 August 2002 *The Daily Star* exclusively revealed that Williams had a secret

ESCAPE AND ESCAPOLOGY

album up his sleeve. "Robbie hasn't just been chilling out in California, but secretly recording his new album." A week later on 17 August *The Sun* announced that the secret album, *Escapology*, would be released on 18 November but as yet Williams hadn't signed a record deal, however "the big four labels – Sony, BMG, Warner and Universal – are battling with his old label EMI to secure him."

Universal was tipped as the favourite to get Williams' signature as it was believed he was unhappy with the way he had been promoted by EMI in the US.

Williams used *Escapology* in his negotiations with all the big players – he was in a great position. He had created a quality piece of work – it was very slick and sounded great and many thought it was his best album to date. Very shrewdly Williams had it on hand to play and tease record executives with – it had obvious commercial success written all over it and they were all chomping at the bit. Letting music journalists have exclusive tasters of the album tracks was another tactical move that paid off – as they wrote about it enthusiastically, whetting the public's appetite. *The Sunday People* newspaper even had an exclusive picture of the album's cover – with Williams suspended in mid-

ESCAPE AND ESCAPOLOGY

air, upside-down in a straight-jacket, just like Houdini, as early as 15 September 2002. Reminiscent of football transfer auctions, with figures as big as telephone numbers being bandied about, it was believed in August that Williams would sign a deal worth as much as £75 million with one of EMI's rivals. This deal would include a share of merchandising and tour revenue for the record label, which had never happened before.

On 2 October 2002 after much speculation Williams signed with his old label EMI in a record-breaking deal worth an estimated £80 million. It was the second biggest deal in music history (Michael Jackson held the first, he signed with Sony in 1991 for a staggering $623 million, until Williams' deal Whitney Houston held second place, she signed a contract worth an estimated £70 million with Arista in 2001) and had Williams declaring to the nation that he was "rich beyond my wildest dreams".

Copies were being reserved in their thousands online by the likes of *Amazon* before a deal had even been signed because a definite release date had been announced by Williams' management team, IE Music. When *Escapology* was actually released – exactly as planned on 18 November (and

ESCAPE AND ESCAPOLOGY

just in time to catch Christmas shoppers) – it went straight into the album charts at number one and became the fastest and biggest selling album of the year – when it had only been in the shops for six weeks.

Some financial analysts believe, however, that the figure of £80million has been exaggerated. CNN News noted on the day the deal with EMI was announced (2 October) that although share prices in EMI Group Plc had initially climbed by five per cent when the deal was first announced, they had fallen to a rise of one per cent by the close of business. Reuters news reports also confirmed that some analysts believed the deal to be exaggerated.

Whatever the actual amount it can safely be said that it was huge and was enough to secure Williams with EMI for the foreseeable future, the same could not, however, be said for Guy Chambers. Before the ink was even dry on the contract rumours broke out that Chambers had not been secured for the four albums Williams had signed up for – he had co-written 12 tracks with Williams on *Escapology*, but beyond that nothing had been formally agreed. While he had been working with Williams he hadn't done so on an exclusive basis, and had been incredibly busy writing and producing

ESCAPE AND ESCAPOLOGY

for other artists. He had worked with Will Young and wrote *Lover Won't You Stay* for his album; worked with Shaznay Lewis (ex-vocalist from All Saints) on her solo album; he had produced *Life and Love: The Very Best of Diana Ross*; had collaborated with Cathy Dennis, among other songwriters and had worked on two film soundtracks – *Bridget Jones' Diary* and *A Knight's Tale*. When Williams signed with EMI, Chambers had a lot of other projects pencilled in that he planned to work on. He particularly wanted to work with a new girl band called The Licks – and had made no secret of the fact that he enjoyed working with lots of different artists.

While working with Williams, Chambers had co-written the majority of the material on all of his five albums and had also co-produced them with Steve Power, and if that wasn't enough he was also musical director of his live band. A few days after Williams signed with EMI, Chambers (who had his own, separate contract with EMI) issued a statement which declared that although the past six years had been a fantastic white knuckle ride and that he was extremely proud of what he and Williams had achieved, it was time to move on to other things.

ROBBIE WILLIAMS

ESCAPE AND ESCAPOLOGY

Williams' statement was more brief, stating "Our relationship has terminated." It is believed that the collaboration ended because he would not agree to work exclusively with Williams. On 8 October 2002, *Music Week* reported that Tim Clark had confirmed that Chambers had been dropped, but gave no indication as to the reason for the split. *Music Week*, however, noted that the reason for Chambers' dismissal was because he had wanted some money in recognition of the success of *Escapology*, but that EMI and Williams refused.

There has been much speculation since the split about whether Williams will be able to deliver material as good as the songs he wrote with Chambers – the few songs that Williams penned on his own, including *Nan's Song* for *Escapology*, indicate that he won't be all at sea without Chambers . Although it is recognised that Williams is an excellent lyricist, Chambers did use his musical expertise – writing the music to accompany the songs – to great effect and he had the ability to turn Williams' songs into hits, using his magic touch or what the journalist Adrian Deevoy has called "sprinkling his fairy dust" over the raw material. Whether Williams finds someone that he clicks with and writes so well

Robbie Williams (bottom left) joined Take That at the age of 15. Take That's blend of high energy disco tunes and slow melodic ballards proved a great success and in 1993 they had three consecutive number ones with: 'Pray', 'Relight my Fire' and 'Babe' amongst numerous other hits. Robbie left the band in 1995.

Take That: Gary Barlow (top left), Jason Orange (top middle), Howard Donald (far right), Mark Owen (bottom right).

Since the release of Robbie's single 'Angels' in December 1997 his solo career has gone from strength to strength. Other hits include: 'Millennium', 'She's the One' and 'Rock DJ' that all reached the number one spot.

In August 2003 Robbie performed to over 1.5 million fans on his 'Weekends of Mass Destruction' tour across Europe. The UK leg broke all attendance records at Knebworth with three consecutive sell-out gigs.

The 2003 'Weekends of Mass Destruction' tour saw Robbie performing in 20 countries. At the start of the show Robbie was lowered above the stage on two cable winches, tied upside down like Houdini, from here he would wriggle free before launching into his first number. Usually, the aptly named 'Let me Entertain You'.

ESCAPE AND ESCAPOLOGY

with, only time will tell. The good news is that Williams isn't short of a bob or two, so he should be able to hire the best people to work with.

As Williams' lyrics are always so full of personal meaning it is no surprise that everyone was keen to know why he'd entitled his fifth album *Escapology* – who or what was he escaping from. Some newspapers even thought it was still Take That, but Williams had really moved on by 2002. Williams said he decided upon the title while driving around in Hollywood thinking about Houdini. When pressed on whether the title had any meaning he told the Scottish newspaper, The Daily Record that there was no real meaning attached to the title. He stated that he no longer wanted to escape from that thing that was Robbie Williams, instead he felt that he had escaped from being so self-critical and damning about his work and in fact, was now proud of and happy with it

While working on *Escapology*, Williams had been having doubts about his material and wanted to recreate himself. Sometime during the production of this album he turned a corner and started to enjoy what he was doing once again and became positive about the whole process. In November 2002 in an interview Williams revealed that he had been suffering from depression and it is likely that having treatment for depression is what turned Williams' world around for him.

He talked candidly in various interviews about what it is like to suffer from the illness. He made reference to people's perception of him – that he was weird, after all what did a rich, successful and very handsome young man have to be depressed about? Williams agreed that they were right and that there were no reasons for him to be depressed, but explained that the illness wasn't an excuse to moan about his life. The medication he was taking made him feel as if he had a constant flu-like bug and although he wouldn't need the pills forever, he was making sure he closed the stable door before the horse bolted.

In freeing himself – whether it was from his own personal demons, the media gaze in the UK, or whatever – Williams was able to write an album that he is really proud of – and sign with EMI to write four more, which is enough to be getting on with. When *Feel*, the first single from *Escapology*, was released in December 2002 Williams hadn't had a single out on his own for over a year (he had featured on guest vocals on *My Culture* with One Giant Leap in April 2002) – so it was a long awaited return to the charts. *Feel* peaked at number two and while a disappointment in that it didn't provide Williams with his second consecutive Christmas number one, it did very well when you realise that *Escapology* was running out of the shops at the same time, achieving record sales.

Williams has so far released four singles from *Escapology,* and while he is immediately recognisable as the artist in each of them and they could all be described as 'classic Robbie Williams', they are also all very different from each other. This contests to the fact that Williams' range has definitely expanded since he went solo, and that he can cover many genres with great aplomb. He can do the introspective ballad, the rock anthem, the euphoric love song that makes the hair on the back of your neck stand up – and still get his videos banned!

Pure pop at its best, *Feel* was the obvious choice as a single from *Escapology*. It is very polished with incredibly strong, gutsy vocals and as soon as you hear the first two lines of the chorus you're hooked, this one really is classic Robbie Williams! In an interview Williams stated: "The song has a very simple message – that if I fall in love with somebody my world will be correct. I

ESCAPE AND ESCAPOLOGY

don't think that is necessarily the truth, but we shall see!" His second single *Come Undone* (released in April 2003, reached number four) is a completely different kettle of fish. Its lyrics are raw, honest, insecure and acutely personal. While exploring his 'drugs hell' yet again it still has the power to shock – which was certainly the case with the video. Not many people will have seen it because it was banned for being too sexually explicit by most broadcasters before it was ever shown publicly. It's always good for a singer's credibility once their material has been banned and it's free publicity.

His third single release from the album was *Something Beautiful* (released in July 2003). A complete juxtaposition from *Come Undone*, it is a mellow, slow burner and once it gets under your skin it is hard to shake it. It reiterates the message of *Feel* – but in a quieter, more altruistic way – that if you find love then it will sort you out.

Turning away from the loved-up feel of *Something Beautiful*, *Sexed Up* (released in November 2003) is harsh and bitter. Much press coverage has indicated that this was the song Williams wrote when he broke up with former All Saints singer, Nicole Appleton. Whatever its

ESCAPE AND ESCAPOLOGY

origins, it uses clever lyrics that mix anger and fake nonchalance to tell of a bitter break-up.

Other highlights on the album include two big anthems for those big stadium tours *Love Somebody* and *Monsoon*, but best of all is *Revolution*, which features gospel singer Rose Stone on guest vocals. The song is about redemption and coming to terms with your own failings – to accept your past and then leave it behind. With *Escapology,* Williams has created a mature and fresh sounding album that doesn't dwell too much on his troubled past – and it can only be hoped that he is at last laying his demons to rest. A Greatest Hits album is expected around Christmas 2004, and with two new albums, without Guy Chambers, commissioned by EMI after that – Williams has everything to play for.

8

Live floor show

I magine a stomping, gyrating, sweating bundle of energy that can belt out rock anthems, bear his soul in slow and moving ballads and croon with the best of them while keeping up a constant banter with the audience – combining vulnerability and cocksure arrogance at the same time. Add to the mix a 100,000-strong crowd who know every word to every song – and you come close to the Robbie Williams live experience. His voice has a hidden power that grows in range, volume and intensity when he performs and it just seems to get better as his confidence grows during a live show. When you're watching him you get completely caught up in

LIVE FLOOR SHOW

his act and for the 95 minutes or so of the performance he can do no wrong. Singing live is what he does best and he knows it. His fans love his polished singles with their clever and funny videos, but no where near as much as the real thing – when Williams is raw and uncut he is adored.

Throughout 2003 Williams was to prove that he could pack out every major stadium in Europe, but he has always been fond of small, intimate venues and often sneaks in a small gig before or after he embarks upon a major tour. For example, on 4 September 2000 he performed at London's Scala in a special performance for *BBC Radio 1* competition winners and completed a full set which included *Let Me Entertain You, Better Man, Angels* and *Kids* with Kylie Minogue. This gig preceded his UK tour that started the following month. In October 2002, Williams performed a small gig at Pinewood Studios in front of only 400 fans for a BBC special – choosing this as his first gig after signing his £80 million record deal with EMI. It was also the first time he had performed live since his hugely successful swing concert at the Albert Hall. He included the tracks *Strong, Have You Met Miss Jones, One For My Baby, Feel, Supreme* and *Nan's Song* in his performance.

ROBBIE WILLIAMS

LIVE FLOOR SHOW

Williams has played hundreds of live gigs to millions of fans worldwide, but his most critically acclaimed performances have been those in front of a home crowd in the UK and Ireland. These include Glastonbury 1998, his 2000 UK Tour (unofficially entitled The Sermon On The Mount Tour); Slane Castle, Ireland August 1999; Live at the Albert Hall, August 2001; and his Weekends of Mass Distraction European Tour (July – November 2003) – the highlights of which were to be three concerts at Knebworth Park.

Following on from his success at the Brits in February 1998, when he performed his infamous duet with Tom Jones to great acclaim, Williams played at Glastonbury on Saturday 27 June 1998 and exorcised many of his personal demons. On the central Pyramid Stage – the same place he had sung with Oasis in 1995 and which proved to be the catalyst to his break up with Take That – Williams finally proved that he could hack it in the major league. Over 100,000 revellers braved the weather – rain turned much of the site into a muddy quagmire – to welcome Williams on stage. During the weekend he shared the bill with Blur, Pulp, Underworld, Catatonia, Nick Cave and The Bad Seeds, The Foo Fighters, James, Spiritualized and

LIVE FLOOR SHOW

the Lightening Seeds among others. Out of the money raised at the festival over £500,000 went to Greenpeace, Oxfam and Water Aid. That year Williams got the festival bug and in addition to playing at Glastonbury he played at T-in-the Park in Glasgow and the V-98 Festival, he also supported The Verve at Slane Castle in Ireland.

In 1999 Williams undertook a 25-date arena tour, visiting 13 cities throughout the UK and Ireland. During that tour he headlined Slane Castle and tickets for the event sold out five weeks before the gig, faster than any other acts that had headlined there – including David Bowie, Queen, Bruce Springsteen, REM and The Verve. This stadium gig was webcast live to over 50,000 Internet viewers and is the subject matter of one of Williams' early DVD's *Where Egos Dare* (released in November 2000).

In 2000, Williams embarked upon his second major UK tour unofficially known as The Sermon On The Mount Tour and demonstrated for the first time that he could carry off a huge stadium tour on the power of his voice and personality alone (and a few fireworks). He did not employ parades of dancers or indulge himself in loads of costume changes and apart from Kylie, who accompanied him at many of the gigs to sing their hit, *Kids,* Williams was alone on stage with just his band and backing singers and sold out every gig he played to rave reviews. Performing throughout October and into November 2000 he covered the length and breadth of the country. He kicked off at the NEC in Birmingham on 10 October to 10,000 fans. At the end of the tour, when he'd injured his back, had flu and was shattered, he employed his stiff upper lip and ensured that his show went on. His last two gigs on 6 and 7 November in London's Dockland's (to 16,000 fans each night) were the best of the tour. His set included *Better Man, The Road To Mandalay, Forever Texas, Let Love Be Your Energy, She's The One, My Way* and of course *Angels*, which was sung almost entirely by the crowd. His encore was his thundering punked-up classic, *Rock DJ*.

If Williams was tired at the end of his 2000 tour, he was soon to find out that it was nothing compared to how he would feel after he'd completed his 2001 schedule. His European Tour is the subject of the book *Somebody, Someday* by Robbie Williams and Mark McCrum and the complementary video/DVD, *Nobody Someday*. The tour kicked off on 12 February at the Isstadion, Stockholm and took in

ROBBIE WILLIAMS

LIVE FLOOR SHOW

Copenhagen, Hamburg, Berlin, Dusseldorf, Stuttgart, Nuremburg, Frankfurt, Munich, Paris, Brussels, Rotterdam and Vienna.

He embarked upon his second UK stadium tour in as many years on 6 July 2001 at Dublin's Lansdowne Road. He also played two nights in Cardiff, three at the Milton Keynes Bowl, three nights at Manchester Old Trafford and two at Hampden Park in Glasgow. No sooner had he finished the hard slog of performing at these large stadiums, then he was planning and performing his highly-acclaimed one-off gig of swing hits at the Royal Albert in front of a celebrity-heavy, invited audience. This concert is recorded on his *Live At The Albert* VHS/DVD and shows an altogether different version to the Robbie Williams we are used to. Gone is the strutting, the gyrating and the attitude and in its place can be found a debonair, sophisticated, finger clicking crooner – who continues to enthrall his audience as he captures precisely the swing mood of the Fifties and Sixties – and shows that he can *really* sing.

In the summer of 2003 Williams embarked upon his biggest ever European schedule – the Weekends of Mass Distraction tour. He hadn't toured for two years, as he had moved to LA, so his gigs were highly anticipated events and marked the highlight of his performing career. He performed in 25 huge arenas (often doing two nights at the same venue) in 20 countries to over 1.5 million people, with tickets selling out within a day or two of going on sale.

On site at every concert there were eight massive LED screens – that split into sections – so that Williams could be seen by everyone in the capacity crowds. At the opening of his performance Williams was lowered above the stage on two cable winches, tied up and upside down like Houdini (and himself on the cover of *Escapology*) – from which he wriggles free before launching into his first number – which was usually *Let Me Entertain You*. Throughout every show Williams exuded energy, charisma and professionalism – and was praised to rave reviews in every country he visited. The tour lasted from June to November and took in 25 cities and stadiums. The average capacity crowd was 65,000.

Having been out of the spotlight for a while Williams had a point to prove – that he was the world's best solo performer and to back this up his team booked him in for three consecutive nights at Knebworth (1–3 August 2003). It is the most

LIVE FLOOR SHOW

hallowed of UK concert sites with a massive capacity of 125,000. Led Zeppelin and Oasis both held records for filling this site for two consecutive nights. Some critics believed Williams was being optimistic when he announced his three-night plan, but he had no problems filling the venue – all 375,000 tickets sold out in a record seven hours – with Williams performing the best gigs of his life. UK sales of the resulting album, *Live At Knebworth*, sold 117,863 copies in its first week and have sold over 1 million copies to date. The resulting video *What We Did Last Summer – Robbie Williams Live at Knebworth*, is the fastest selling music DVD ever in the UK.

Williams has proved his point – no other performer can touch him.

9

Mr Entertainment

ROBBIE WILLIAMS

MR ENTERTAINMENT

R obbie Williams is a visual performer – he demands to be seen not just heard – the promotional videos for his singles are witty, clever and timeless and the DVD/video recordings of his live shows continue to be bestsellers months (and sometimes years) after their initial release. This testament to the longevity of 'Williams the artist' has not gone unnoticed by his record label EMI. When Williams signed his record £80million contract in 2002 the deal included a share of merchandising and concert revenue for the record label, the first time a major performer had agreed to such a clause. In addition, it is believed that Williams would have received an initial down payment of around £20 million when he signed the contract and the rest of the revenue would be made up of album sales, merchandising and concert revenue for the duration of his four-album deal. Williams does sell a lot of albums, that is a given, what is unusual about him is the amount of videos and DVDs he actually shifts at the same time – so much so that a large proportion of his future income is based on their sales.

But this isn't a risk for Williams or EMI as the sales of his 2003 video, *What We Did Last Summer – Robbie Williams Live at Knebworth*, demonstrate very clearly. In the UK this DVD is the fastest selling music DVD ever, which isn't such a surprise as Williams is very popular in his home market – but the scale is astonishing, in the first week of its release it sold 48,000 copies alone. Add to this, his international appeal and success and his videos become a license to print money! In its online archive *MTV.com* has recorded just how well this DVD did around the world: it went triple platinum in Australia (outselling the *Lord of the Rings* special edition DVD and *Matrix II*) and Portugal; achieved Gold sales status in Sweden

MR ENTERTAINMENT

and Holland; and went straight in at number one in Austria and Germany (where it sold 18,000 copies on the first day of its release).

The strategy behind Williams' DVDs and videos is two-fold. The first concentrates on his promotional videos for his singles and the second is performance-based, recordings of his live shows (that only a fraction of his fan-base can attend in person) and his specially recorded sessions for DVD. There is even one DVD, *Escape Routes* (released in December 2002), that is only available exclusively from Williams' official website. (It can be found in the 'inner sanctum' section of the site which is only for his registered fans) at www.robbiewilliams.com.

The first stream of video and DVD recordings – the promotional videos for his singles – is probably not as lucrative as his live performances, but is a great record for his fans because once a single serves its time in the charts it is very difficult to see the video again – except in music channel retrospectives, like *MTV* or *VH1* artist specials. Williams' videos are usually very cleverly written and produced, memorable and like his albums, played over and over again. They are often humourous, court some controversy, or get banned – which just adds to their appeal.

ROBBIE WILLIAMS

MR ENTERTAINMENT

Some of his most interesting videos to date, include the following:

Feel – Promoting his first single release from *Escapology*, Williams is a cowboy in this spaghetti-Western stylised video, which features Hollywood actress Daryl Hannah. Williams rides into town with some real-life cowboys (he had to learn to ride a horse for the shoot) and wins the ranch owners girlfriend (Hannah) in an arm-wrestling competition, but not before he strips down and has a bath in a water trough. The video was filmed in the mountains near Calgary in Canada, and was paid for by Williams himself (its estimated cost is £500,000) as he was between record labels at the time the film was made.

She's the One – This is a very funny video that features Williams as a championship ice-skater, in the fashion of Torvill and Dean, and won him a BRIT for Best British Video.

Rock DJ – The video for Rock DJ was given a 15 certificate, so could only be shown in clip-format on some teenage-focused TV programmes, with some broadcasters considering it to be too horrific to be shown in full – this of course elevated its status. It was directed by the video veteran Vaughan Arnell and features Williams on the dance floor trying to attract the attention of the gorgeous female DJ (played by Lauren Gold). He does a striptease becomes completely naked and then starts to peel off layers of his skin and muscle, until all that is left is his dancing skeleton. In the video Williams is objectifying his role as a pop star, declaring if you want a piece of me, then take it. But he is also showing, in his desire to get noticed by the DJ and the beautiful roller-skaters that circle him and ignore him, that he courts attention. *Rock DJ* won a BRIT for Best British Video and an MTV Video Music Award for Best Special Effects, and was also nominated for Best Male Video and Breakthrough Video in America. It was also nominated for a Billboard Video Music Award for Best Clip of the Year in the US. The video was banned in the Dominican Republic as its Commission for Broadcasting believed it contained many elements of Satanism.

Angels – A good DVD for fans of Williams' early solo material as it includes many of his early hits. Naturally it has *Angels*, but also *Lazy Days* and *South of the Border*. Footage of a holiday in Jamaica is the set for the *Heaven From Here* video, *Get the Joke* (filmed backstage at The Forum in London) and *Grace*.

ROBBIE WILLIAMS

MR ENTERTAINMENT

Something Beautiful – A spoof of TV talent shows in the vein of *Pop Idol* and *Fame Academy* and features many young hopefuls trying to be Robbie Williams in front of a panel of judges that include Williams' dad. The three finalists are then treated to the high-life, sampling what it would really be like to be pop stars.

Millennium – Just as the song *Millennium* borrows from John Barry's theme tune to *You Only Live Twice*, so too does Williams in this video when he appears as James Bond. American audiences are continually accused of not getting Williams' irony in the British press, so much so that Williams was asked to change this video for the US market, but he told MTV that he wasn't going to change the video because he didn't believe that the American people really thought he was being serious – he credited them with more intelligence and was proven right.

The video was used to promote *Millennium* in the US and his single made the Billboard Top 10.

Come Undone – Banned in most countries for being too sexually explicit before it was even aired, *Come Undone* was directed by Jonas Akerlund and features Williams participating in an orgy. Williams explained that he had made the video as

MR ENTERTAINMENT

a complete contrast to the beautiful *Feel*, because not everything can be beautiful and that there needed to be snakes and sex – although he admitted that the video was very graphic and perhaps a bit unsettling. In the video he appears to have sex with girls, which changes to look like he is having sex with boys. Williams wanted to put the male stuff in as a response to all the gay stars who pretend to be straight – he jokes about setting up a campaign where straight men pretend to be gay!

Williams' performance-based videos (and DVDs) are less contentious than his promotional material and have become the ideal vehicle for Williams to reach the fans that cannot attend his gigs or are not lucky enough to pick up the handful of tickets available to the public when he performs at small one-off venues. His DVDs often include exclusive material that is unavailable elsewhere, just as his albums always include a hidden track at the end – which ensures that his fans continue to buy them.

One of the first videos Williams ever compiled was of a live show – at The Forum in London on 3 June 1998 and is the subject of *Live In Your Living Room*. It proved to be so successful that it is a model that has been repeated and developed ever since. The video (not available on DVD) includes 15 live tracks from the concert, featuring the likes of *Let Me Entertain You*, *Clean* and *Angels* as well as interviews and behind the scenes coverage.

Where Egos Dare (DVD) was released in November 2000 and covers Williams' concert at Slane Castle in Ireland (August 1999) in front of an 80,000-strong audience. It is a real collectors item as it not only features Williams singing some of his best live material – *Angels*, The Clash's *Should I Stay, Or Should I Go*, *Strong* and *Millennium* – much of the live material is also recorded using multi-camera angles, so the viewer can get interactive and choose what part of the stage it wants to view, plus not having to stick with the director's cut. Behind the scenes material includes rehearsals, sound checks and interviews. This DVD is special because it also includes a documentary on the making of *Sing When You're Winning*; a documentary that goes behind-the-scenes of the *Rock DJ* video; a film entitled *Short Cuts* which gives a short biographical background to Williams' life in video clips; *and Dance With The Devil*, a previously unrecorded song and video.

When Williams broke out of the mould and

MR ENTERTAINMENT

recorded his swing album, *Swing When You're Winning* in November 2001 he promoted it at a one-off concert at the Albert Hall in London on 10 October 2001, in front of an invited audience. The concert was then shown exclusively on BBC1 and is shown again on the video/DVD, *Live At The Albert*. But this isn't just an ordinary concert film; *Live At The Albert* broke all DVD sales records in the UK, with sales of over 140,000 – and a staggering 250,000 when both DVD and video formats are combined. It was also nominated for a Grammy Award for Best Music Video, Long Form. Directed by Hamish Hamilton, *Live At The Albert* is a tribute to Frank Sinatra and the Rat Pack and features Williams singing many Rat Pack classic hits including *Ain't That A Kick In The Head*, *The Lady Is A Tramp*, *Mr Bojangles* and *My Way*. The evening is compered by Rupert Everett and features duets with Jane Horrocks and Williams' best friend, Jonathan Wilkes – they sing *Me And My Shadow*. An unexpected, and crowd-winning highlight of the evening was Williams' posthumous duet via video link with Sinatra himself, singing *It Was a Very Good Year*. Williams' performance is second to none and really illustrates the range of his voice – he was

MR ENTERTAINMENT

born to sing these songs. Added features on this DVD are the documentary, *Well Swung*, which follows Williams to Capitol Studios in LA where he recorded *Swing When You're Winning* with many of the musicians that originally recorded with Frank Sinatra, Dean Martin and Sammy Davis Jr et al.

Nobody, Someday was released in July 2002 and accompanies the book *Somebody, Someday* written by Mark McCrum and Robbie Williams and follows Williams on tour in Europe in 2001. It follows the tour and intersperses live concert coverage with observational footage and in-depth conversations with Williams and his crew. It is very funny and gives a great insight into life on the road with a huge entourage, band and crew.

Williams released two video/DVDs in 1993, the first was *The Robbie Williams Show* (in March 2003) which is set in a fake Sixties studio, and sees Williams talking about his life between singing live in the studio – an imitation of a Sixties' TV special. Some of his featured songs include *Mr Bojangles*, *Have You Met Miss Jones*, *Feel and No Regrets*.

The second was *What We Did Last Summer – Robbie Williams Live at Knebworth*, the fastest selling DVD in UK history. Not only that, it really is

MR ENTERTAINMENT

one of the best concerts he has ever performed and records the highlight of his career, performing three sell-out gigs at Knebworth Park. The concert records Williams in all his glory – with the crowd going wild at his every move, and he even sings *Back For Good* with his old Take That band mate, Mark Owen. DVD extras include the UNICEF film, *More Precious Than Gold* (Williams is an ambassador for Unicef); trailers for his other videos and an interactive game that gives you hidden video clips if you manage to hit a moving on-screen Robbie.

Williams has surpassed all expectations as a performer and his video/DVD sales success are a lasting testament to his popularity and longevity – and they are also a nice little earner on the side!

Robbie Williams – Videography

Live In Your Living Room – VHS only
(November 1998)
Coverage: Filmed during Williams' live concert at The Forum, London, 3 June 1998. Features 15 live tracks, including *Let Me Entertain You, Clean, There She Goes, Killing Me, Angels, Back For Good, Teenage Millionaire, Ego a Go Go, Baby Girl Window and South of the Border.*

ROBBIE WILLIAMS

MR ENTERTAINMENT

Extras: Interviews/behind the scenes coverage
Angels – DVD (December 1999)
Coverage: *Angels, Lazy Days, South of the Border,
Heaven From Here, Get the Joke, Grace*, and
Man Machine.
Extras: Interviews, poems and interactive game

Rock DJ – DVD (July 2000)
Tracks: *Rock DJ* video (uncensored version),
The Making of *Rock DJ*

Where Egos Dare – DVD (November 2000)
Coverage: Film of Williams' concert at Slane
Castle, Ireland in August 1999
Extras: Behind the scenes at the concert, Behind
the scenes of Rock DJ; Sing When You're Winning
(making of the album).
Bonus Track: Dance With The Devil

Somethin' Stupid – DVD (December 2001)
Coverage: *Somethin' Stupid; Let's Face The Music
And Dance* (audio); *That's Life* (audio).
Extras: Photo gallery

Live At The Albert – DVD & VHS (December 2001)
Coverage: Exclusive live film of Williams' Concert

MR ENTERTAINMENT

at the Royal Albert Hall, London on 10 October 2001 – performed and recorded as a tribute to Frank Sinatra and the Rat Pack.

Extras: Pre-show build-up and aftershow coverage. Exclusive to the DVD is the documentary *Well Swung* which follows Williams on his trip to Capitol Studios in LA where he recorded his swing album, Swing When You're Winning.

Nobody Someday – DVD & VHS (July 2002)
Coverage: Documentary to accompany the book *Somebody, Someday*, which charts his European tour in 2001. Exclusive to the DVD is a bonus interactive quiz about the documentary and if you answer the set questions correctly you can view additional material from the tour that didn't make the official film.

Xbox DVD Special (November 2002)
Coverage: *Let Me Entertain You, Angels* (Live from Cologne, Germany) and the Making of *Escapology*. Also features audio *tracks Hot Fudge, Love Somebody, Nobody Someday, Ugly Love* (DVD exclusive) and *Coffee, Tea and Sympathy* (DVD exclusive).

ROBBIE WILLIAMS

MR ENTERTAINMENT

Feel – DVD (December 2002)
Coverage: Feel and out-takes from the making of the Feel video. Also includes two audio tracks: Nobody Someday and You're History.

Escape Routes – DVD (December 2002)
This DVD is only available exclusively from the Robbie Williams Official Website
Coverage: Making of *Escapology*, and *Feel* (audio track).

The Robbie Williams Show – VHS & DVD (March 2003)
Coverage: Live showcase which primarily promotes material *from Sing When You're Winning* and *Escapology*, it is set in a fake Sixties studio as a spoof TV special – with Williams talking about his life between songs. *Features Rock DJ, Have You Met Miss Jones, One For My Baby, Feel, No Regrets and Mr Bojangles.*

Come Undone – DVD single (April 2003)
Coverage: Come Undone and Come Undone Live. Plus audio tracks Happy Easter (War is Coming) and One Fine Day.
Extras: Photo gallery

ROBBIE WILLIAMS

MR ENTERTAINMENT

Something Beautiful – DVD single (July 2003)
Coverage: *Something Beautiful* (interactive video) and audio *tracks Coffee, Tea & Sympathy* and *Berliner Star*.

What We Did Last Summer - Robbie Williams Live at Knebworth 2003 – VHS & DVD (November 2003)
Coverage: Live coverage of Williams' record-breaking Knebworth gigs in August 2003 before 375,000 fans. Consists of two discs, the first includes two hours of live concert coverage and the second is set backstage. Also features Williams singing the old Take That single *Back For Good* with Mark Owen. Includes *Let Me Entertain You, Monsoon, Come Undone, Strong, Kids, Rock DJ* and *Angels*. Also features *More Precious Than Gold* a film made for UNICEF in 2003, which draws attention to child exploitation.

10

Giving something back

ROBBIE WILLIAMS

GIVING SOMETHING BACK

Much has been made of Williams' wealth, but his career hasn't been just about making money, it has been more about proving himself as a credible artist and performer. That done, Williams has worked with several charitable organisations to raise money – in particular UNICEF, Comic Relief, Jeans for Genes and The Anthony Nolan Bone Marrow Trust. He has also set up his own charity, Give It Sum, to tackle poverty and social injustice in the UK. He started the project in his home town of Stoke-on-Trent and has so far raised money for and donated over £1.5

GIVING SOMETHING BACK

million to charities in the North Staffordshire area.

Williams has had strong links with the United Nations children's fund, UNICEF since 1998, when he was asked to support and promote the Music for UNICEF initiative by the late Ian Dury, who was then the UNICEF UK Special Representative to the Music Industry. Williams agreed and joined Dury on a trip to Sri Lanka to see some of its children being immunised against polio. It is important to have celebrity backing for events like this because it drums up lots of media attention – and makes campaigns that are often ignored by the press top of the news agenda, providing them with more publicity than they could ever generate on their own. In turn, it is hoped that the attention attracted to a cause will encourage donations, from individuals and more importantly governments and private industry that have a lot more to give.

Since his first visit to Sri Lanka, Williams has been associated with UNICEF. In May 2000 he travelled to Mozambique to draw attention to the way HIV/AIDS has ravaged the population, there are now 500,000 AIDS orphans in Mozambique alone (UNICEF estimates the worldwide figure of AIDS orphans to be 13 million)

GIVING SOMETHING BACK

many of who are also infected. In December of the same year he helped UNICEF launch their Break The Silence Campaign – to break the silence about the continued and escalating spread of AIDS. The campaign was centred around UNICEF's website where they had constructed a figurative wall of silence which could be knocked down, brick by brick, as more people signed up to support the campaign on their website. To support and promote the launch of the event Williams literally knocked down a wall in east London with a demolition ball. The event took place on 1 December 2000, World AIDS Day. In 2003, Williams helped produce a film for UNICEF UK. Entitled *More Precious Than Gold*, the film is presented and narrated by Williams and draws attention to child exploitation and trafficking often for sex or hard labour. *More Precious Than Gold* is featured in its entirety on Williams' record breaking *DVD What We Did Last Summer – Robbie Williams Live at Knebworth*. It was played at every concert during Williams' 2003 Weekends of Mass Distraction Tour of Europe and because of Williams' involvement in the film; it was shown every day during the summer of 2003 on music channels MTV and VH1.

GIVING SOMETHING BACK

UNICEF believes that "children are the cornerstones of human progress" and was created (in December 1946) to overcome the obstacles that poverty, violence, disease and discrimination place in a child's path. More information on the work of UNICEF is available at www.unicef.org.

When Williams helped to raise money for Comic Relief in the late Nineties he became aware of the ways in which charitable monies are accrued and distributed – and how the costs of running a charity often eats into much of what is raised. He admired the way in which Comic Relief managed to redistribute all of what it raised in its name back out into the projects it supported, and how it championed many charities within the UK as well as abroad. Uncannily, this 'charity begins at home' policy often encourages more people to donate money as they believe that in distributing the aid at home as well as abroad it has a direct impact on the lives of people around them, which in turn is much easier to relate to and give to. In addition, Comic Relief's method of revisiting countries or topics e.g. AIDS, to show exactly what past donations have paid for and how much things cost, provides a concrete and finite explanation of how its money is spent. This encourages people to donate more

GIVING SOMETHING BACK

because they can see that it being spent on something real. Williams picked up on this ethos and used it when he launched his own charity, Give It Sum, in 2000 with the help of Comic Relief.

When Williams appeared in an advert for *Pepsi* in 2000 he decided to donate his fee, believed to be £2 million, to charity. He donated some of it to UNICEF, some to Great Ormond Street Hospital and a range of other charities and some to a charity he was setting up himself. *Give It Sum* was set up to help tackle poverty, disadvantage and discrimination, primarily within the UK (and abroad in time). It was set up to support local communities – working with community groups, self-help groups and other local organisations – to improve the lives of people living with poverty through projects that benefited them in the long term, not just quick fixes or cash injections, the benefits of which disappear rapidly. In a press statement at the launch of the charity, Williams noted "the whole point of the fund is to tackle some of the problems associated with poverty and to address some of the social injustices in the world... I'd like to give people... a chance to do something for themselves... It's great to know that every application is visited and thoroughly discussed to make sure that money is spent well and really will make a difference." In the early days the work of Give It Sum was focused on William's home town of Stoke-on-Trent (and the surrounding North Staffordshire area), making a difference to the lives of people from his own community. Since then it has developed to incorporate the work of many local organisations around the UK. So far approximately £1.5 million has gone into funding over 80 community projects that include: a local play scheme for disabled and able-bodied children to play together; a donation of 15 computers to a local community group; a fruit and vegetable company set up by a homeless group to deliver fresh produce to urban areas with few shops; the development of an estate community centre in an old derelict house and a local rape crisis centre. Williams also donated some money to improve library facilities in his old school, St. Margaret Ward RC High School, Tunstall, Stoke-on-Trent and donated £10,000 from the Give It Sum fund to North Staffordshire's Lesbian, Gay and Bisexual Switchboard.

To help fund Give It Sum, Williams famously auctioned a lot of his personal memorabilia in

ROBBIE WILLIAMS

GIVING SOMETHING BACK

April 2001 at Sotheby's – the auction was entitled Bid It Sum. A further online auction on www.sothebys.com raised more money for the fund. It is estimated that both auctions raised around £250,000. Under the hammer went his original hand-written lyrics to *Angels* (which raised a staggering £27,000); the leather jacket he wore for his BRITs duet with Tom Jones in February 1998 (£2,700); the ice-skating outfit he wore in *She's The One* video (£6,500); a pair of Robbie Williams concert tickets (raised £3,000); platinum Take That discs; the jet pack used in his *Millennium* video and his autographed bed (believed to be from Heals it went for £15,400 – it was on sale again on eBay in April 2004).

In addition to the above, Williams has contributed time and effort to support the following charities:

Comic Relief
Williams has continued to raise money for Comic Relief and its associated charities throughout his performing career. In 2003, he made a legendary appearance in the nude to make an appeal for the charity, on BBC TV during Red Nose Day.

ROBBIE WILLIAMS

GIVING SOMETHING BACK

Jeans for Genes Appeal

He is a patron of the Jeans for Genes Appeal – a national campaign which raises money for five national charities that help children with genetic disorders. The campaign works by encouraging everyone to wear jeans to work for one day – usually in October – and pay £1 to the Jeans for Genes appeal for the privilege.

Anthony Nolan Trust

Williams has done a lot of work to support leukemia charities and signed up as a potential bone marrow donor at the Anthony Nolan Trust in 2001. The Anthony Nolan Trust is the main bone marrow register in the UK; anyone can register to donate bone marrow by giving a blood sample to the register and agreeing to donate bone marrow if matched with an existing or future patient. Over 300,000 people in the UK have signed up to the register.

Johnny Herbert Karting Challenge

This charity was set up by the racing drivers fan club – Johnny Herbert has won three Formula One Grand Prix and has also won at Le Mans – it raises money for the National Kidney Research

Fund by organising an annual go-kart race. Many celebrities, including Williams take part in the go-kart race to raise money for the charity.

Everyman Campaign – Fighting Testicular Cancer

To raise awareness about testicular cancer and the importance of men having themselves checked out, Williams took part in his first television commercial in 1999. He appeared in the advert wearing strap-on breasts and told a hand-held video camera that if men took as much notice of their testicles as they did about women's breasts then they needn't suffer unnecessarily from testicular cancer. There is a massive 96 per cent recovery rate from testicular cancer if men are treated early – to do this many taboos have to be broken down – and it was believed that someone of Williams' youth and high profile supporting the campaign would raise awareness. Williams' participation in the advert attracted a great deal of press coverage and publicity.

CancerBACUP

In September 2000, music photographer Hamish Brown published a book of photographs of Williams – exploring his career up to the release of his second album, *I've Been Expecting You* – and included many unpublished images in his collection. The book, entitled *Robbie Williams Photographs*, was published to raise money for the charity CancerBACUP.

Prince's Trust

In 2003 Williams joined many other 'A' list celebrities to support the Prince's Trust charity by participating in the Fashion Rocks extravaganza at the Albert Hall in London. Guests at the event paid £250 for tickets to the fashion show – hosted by Liz Hurley – to watch celebrities like Robbie Williams, Beyonce Knowles, Duncan James (from Blue), Sharleen Spiteri and Sheryl Crowe wear designer clothes. Williams wore a Versace outfit and also performed at the event.

The Prince's Trust is supported by Prince Charles and works towards helping young people – aged 14-30 – to improve their lives through practical support which includes training, mentoring and financial assistance.

11

Ladies, feuds and fallouts

ROBBIE WILLIAMS

LADIES, FEUDS AND FALLOUTS

Robbie Williams is one of the most eligible bachelors in the world – he's young, good-looking and wealthy. He has homes in LA, London and Staffordshire and is rumoured to have bought a country pile in the Sussex countryside (in April 2004). After celebrating his 30th birthday in Scotland with his family and friends he is said to have looked at properties there too. Unfortunately, he has had less luck with the ladies than he's had with his pop career – and has said on several occasions that he wants to settle down and have children. Songs like *Better Man*,

LADIES, FEUDS AND FALLOUTS

Feel and *Something Beautiful* all settle on the same theme – that once he finds love he will be complete. Williams has everything – he just needs someone to share it with.

Once Take That had hit the big time, Nigel Martin-Smith discouraged all of the group from having girlfriends, he did not want his five young prodigies to be distracted from the business of making pop music. Since the group's break-up most of Take That – Williams, Mark Owen and Howard Donald – have all declared that they did date women during their Take That days but that they had to keep it quiet. They kept it so quiet that it was never reported in the press, so to all intents and purposes Take That remained single through-out their recording careers – which is why, when he went solo, Williams' new girlfriend always made the tabloid headlines – it was like forbidden fruit. Although he was the only member of Take That to appear in public with a girlfriend, he dated and appeared in public with the actress Samantha Beckinsale just before the group split-up, his first 'grown-up' girlfriend was big news – especially because she was a Lady.

Williams began dating Lady Jacqueline Hamilton-Smith in late-1995 after they met at a party in Manchester. She is the daughter of Sonia and Lord Colwyn and grew up in Gloucestershire and London, attending public school. She was a make-up artist and seven years older than Williams. Although they kept their relationship under wraps for four months before going on holiday together to Barbados and being pestered by the paparazzi, their relationship was serious. Hamilton-Smith moved in with Williams early on, and they were together for over a year. Williams, however, was only just getting a taste of freedom when they met and when his first three singles failed to hit the number one slot he began to feel the pressure (*Old Before I Die*, number two; *Lazy Days*, number eight; *South of the Border*, number fourteen). Their split, a year later, was blamed by Robbie on the pressures of work. Hamilton-Smith married the actor Sean Pertwee a couple of years later.

Since then he has been linked with the actress Anna Friel, Melanie Chisholm (ex-Spice Girl, Sporty Spice), Andrea Corr (lead singer with The Corrs) and the TV presenter Tania Strecker. Williams has always claimed that he was only just good friends with Anna Friel and that they hung out with each other when they were both vulnerable –

she had just split up with musical entertainer Darren Day at the same time that Williams was coming out of his relationship with Hamilton-Smith. Whether they actually had a relationship is irrelevant because the press hounded them. They had been declared the new celebrity couple, and every time they went out together a photograph was taken and it appeared in the tabloids the next morning. Although neither Williams nor Friel courted the media attention, the connection with each other did neither of them any harm.

Williams is also believed to have been close to Melanie Chisholm and in his attempts to woo Andrea Corr, he sent her 1000 red roses with the message "what can I do to make you love me" (the lyrics of The Corrs hit single of the same title).

He dated television presenter Tania Strecker for approximately three months in 2000 (she is the step-daughter of his manager David Enthoven) – they were mates before their liaison, and although their relationship was short lived, they remain close friends today. Having sung duets with Kylie Minogue and Nicole Kidman there was inevitably some suggestion at the time of each recording that Williams was seeing each of his co-singers, especially as he got on well with both of them and they hung out socially together – but any romantic links have been unfounded.

One of the most prolific relationships in Williams' life to date – in terms of the amount of attention it has attracted – is with Nicole Appleton. Formerly a vocalist with the all-girl band the All Saints, and now in the eponymous band Appleton with her sister Natalie, Nicole Appleton met Williams whilst promoting All Saints' second single, *Never Ever* on the set of a television programme in late-1997. Although he attended her birthday party in October that year they didn't meet up again properly until December 1997 when both Williams and All Saints appeared at the Princess Diana Concert for the Hope benefit gig in Battersea Park, London (where Williams sang *Let It Be* with Gary Barlow). They started dating that month but it didn't become public knowledge until Appleton was spotted by the paparazzi leaving Williams' flat in Notting Hill, London on 2 January 1998 – then the whole world knew about their relationship. They dated for over a year, were engaged twice and finally called it a day in mid-1999. Appleton went on to meet and have a child with Liam Gallagher, lead singer of the band Oasis and

LADIES, FEUDS AND FALLOUTS

a former friend of Williams.

When Williams and Appleton broke up in 1999, as far as everyone was concerned that was the end of their relationship. It wasn't until Nicole and Natalie Appleton wrote their autobiography, *Together*, and it was serialised in consecutive weeks in the October 2002 issues of *Hello* magazine (the book was published in November 2002) that the public became aware of the greater tragedy in their relationship. Appleton had been pregnant with Williams' child and had an abortion in New York in 1999.

Appleton has said she regretted her decision. She states in her book that Williams was supportive of her decision at the time and helped her cope with the aftermath of the operation and her ensuing depression.

Appleton told Williams that she was going to include the information that she had aborted his child in her autobiography before publication and Williams has noted that he thought she was brave in her decision. There appeared to be no hard feelings between Williams and Appleton in 2002 – Williams first stated in an interview for Radio 1 (and in other interviews since) that he had made up with Liam Gallagher and wished both

LADIES, FEUDS AND FALLOUTS

Appleton and Gallagher well in their relation-ship together – before this time. Then in September 2003, Williams released the single *Sexed Up*, which is believed to be about his break-up with Appleton. Williams wrote the song soon after his final break-up with Appleton and his decision to release it as a single almost four years after writing it and just after the publication of her book is very telling. The lyrics are bitter and angry – and indicate that Williams was not happy about Appleton going public about something so personal.

As Williams' love life has always been a topic of press scrutiny, it is no surprise that they had a field day when he became friends with ex-Spice girl, Geri Halliwell. Halliwell's rise to fame was similar to Williams' – she had been part of a five-piece all-girl band who had experienced massive success – at home and abroad – the only difference being that The Spice Girls broke in to the US market when Take That did not. Like Williams, Halliwell was unhappy in the group and was the first to leave amid much publicity and set up her own solo career. To the press theirs was a match made in heaven – pictures of them on a beach holiday in France seemed to tell the tale of two

LADIES, FEUDS AND FALLOUTS

young lovers having the time of their lives. In reality, Williams and Halliwell found solace with each other from their turbulent lives and became really close friends. Halliwell even laughed at the insinuations about their friendship when she presented Williams with a Best British Male award at the Brits in 2001, when she announced "the winner is healthy, talented and according to press reports giving me one." Halliwell has always maintained that she only ever had a friendship with Williams, while Williams has stated that they slept together. Apparently, this difference of opinion is the reason they are no longer friends.

Williams' most recent relationship was with Rachel Hunter. Hunter, originally from New Zealand, was a successful model when she met and married Rod Stewart in 1990, at the age of 21. They had two children together before splitting up in 1999 – she has since returned to her modelling career and lives in LA. Williams and Hunter started seeing each other early in 2002, having been introduced by Williams' friend Ashley Hamilton (son of George and Alana Hamilton, and formerly Rod Stewart's step-son when he was married to Alana). *The News of the World* published raunchy pictures of the couple, semi-

LADIES, FEUDS AND FALLOUTS

naked beside an LA pool, kissing and cuddling. In his book *Robbie Williams, Angels and Demons* the author Paul Scott declares that the whole exercise was a publicity stunt. The pictures were presented to the press as paparazzi shots, taken beside an LA hotel pool without permission being granted by either Williams or Hunter. Scott believes that the photographer had to be very close to the couple to produce the high quality photographs that appeared *in The News of the World* – too close to go unnoticed by the subjects of the photographs. In the light of these revelations, the nature of their relationship has also been questioned. Many of the unsolicited photographs that did appear of the couple in the press during their relationship – at baseball games and low-key restaurants – do confirm the fact that they did have a close friendship at the very least. It is probable that they were together as a couple during this period and the LA pool incident may just have been a stunt that backfired. Hunter told *Hello* magazine in an exclusive interview at the end of 2002, that they had parted as friends after the pressures of work drove them apart.

Williams still lives in LA and London and has yet to find his perfect mate.

ROBBIE WILLIAMS

LADIES, FEUDS AND FALLOUTS

The Gallagher feud

Williams became friends with Liam and Noel Gallagher in 1995 when he broke ranks with Take That and turned up at the Glastonbury festival on his own – and appeared on stage with Oasis. He was in awe of the band – they were making the type of music he wanted to be part of. Their apparent coolness only served to emphasise how un-hip Take That were and fuelled his unhappiness in the group. Williams did however, become friends with the band and was often seen in the company of Liam – especially when he was dating Jacqui Hamilton-Smith, as she was a close friend of Patsy Kensit, Liam Gallagher's then girlfriend (later to become his wife). In early 1998 some ill-feeling between Williams and the Gallagher brothers began to trickle out into the press with Williams stating he was a better live performer than Oasis and Oasis becoming prickly when asked about Williams' change of fortune. Sean Smith in his book *Robbie: The Biography* believes that Williams' burgeoning success was probably the catalyst to the fall-out between Williams and the Gallagher brothers.

He comments on how the early Take

LADIES, FEUDS AND FALLOUTS

That Robbie was no threat to Oasis, but once he had become the multiple award-winning superstar, he also probably became the band's greatest competitor.

Whether Oasis saw Williams as a threat to their popularity is a matter of conjecture – it is unlikely that they would have given Williams' early material enough credence to offer up any constructive comparison with their own work – they probably just thought they were better. Although the root of their fall-out is unclear, its repercussions were widely reported and relished by the press and public alike. The Gallagher's made constant reference to Williams' weight (its fluctuating state has been well documented) with Noel Gallagher referring to Williams as 'the fat dancer from Take That' in *Heat* magazine. Williams, on the other hand, made constant reference to Oasis' music, indicating that their sound had been borrowed from other bands. It is believed that Liam Gallagher made the first reference to beating up Williams privately, with Williams taking his threat into the public area at the Brits in 1999 when he challenged Liam Gallagher to a boxing match. Unsurprisingly a fight never took place, with both sides realising

12

The future

ROBBIE WILLIAMS

THE FUTURE

Robbie Williams turned 30 in February 2004. Having grown up in the public gaze, since he joined Take That at the tender age of 15, he has achieved so much that it is difficult to know where he can go from here.

The only market Williams has yet to crack is America – it is the biggest in the world and it takes a lot of footwork to even get a foothold in, to date Williams has only achieved moderate success there. In 1999 he released his US album, *The Ego Has Landed*, a compilation of the best bits from his first two albums released elsewhere – *Life Thru a Lens* and *I've Been Expecting You*. Although the

THE FUTURE

album made little impression on the Billboard charts, *Millennium* broke into the Top 10 of the Billboard singles charts in June 1999 and *Angels* into the Top 40 in October of the same year. In September 2000 he was nominated for a Billboard Video Music Award for *Rock DJ* and in February 2003 was nominated for a Grammy Award for Best Music Video, Long Play for *Live At The Albert*.

Unlike the UK and much of Europe that have a national system of press, radio and television coverage the US is split up into individual markets. Each major city will have several radio networks which all play different types of music, with very few targeting a national or mixed-genre audience. One of the unique attributes of Williams' music is the fact that it is difficult to pigeon-hole into one category. While this has worked very well for him in Europe, providing him with a huge and varied audience, it stands against him in the US, so his music often gets left off playlists.

The same is true of television and newspapers. Different TV networks air in different areas of the country and there is a larger choice of channels available. Add to that the fact that there is no national press system. For example, *The New York Times, Washington Post, LA Times* all cover certain

THE FUTURE

areas, so to get press coverage a lot more interviews have to be conducted than in the UK, where a single interview in one of the tabloids, will be accessible throughout the country. For any artist to be successful in the US they have to work incredibly hard, virtually having to start all over again. Williams has stated in many interviews that he's made his money already and can now sit back and relax, but whether Williams is willing to do this is open to debate.

There are three schools of thought on the topic. The first is that Williams moved to LA because his fame, in the UK particularly, made it difficult for him to lead a normal life. To be forever in the public gaze takes its toll and causes a great deal of stress to the celebrity, everyone deserves an element of privacy. Williams has stated in many newspaper and magazine interviews that he loves the fact that he can walk down a street in the US and go virtually unrecognised – he finds it very liberating and enjoyable. If Williams does crack the US he may well lose a lot of this anonymity. In recent years he has also become a lot more concerned about his personal security – living in LA as a small fish in a big pond has the benefit of being safer especially as it is normal to have million-pound security systems surrounding a property.

The second school of thought is that Williams cannot be bothered to crack America – it is too much hard work – a belief backed up by Williams himself in an interview with VH1 in April 2003, when he says that he is quite happy having a successful career everywhere else in the world except the States. He is aware that the US market is a very difficult nut to crack and that it takes a lot of very hard work. Williams goes on to talk about how he worked very hard to achieve his commercial success and became very ill doing it, adding that he doesn't want to work that hard again. He finishes by saying that it will be great if success happens and if it doesn't then that's okay too.

The third belief is that Williams' apparent bravado about his lack of success is false, that his ego is too big to allow him go relatively unnoticed in a country as big as the US. Some observers believe that written into his contract with EMI was a clause that ensured the record company pulls out all the stops in the future to ensure Williams is promoted to the best of their ability with any new album releases. Only time will tell which theory is right – and in reality it will probably be a mixture of all three.

ROBBIE WILLIAMS

THE FUTURE

As part of the record contract he signed with EMI in 2002, Williams agreed to produce three more albums. It is believed that the first of these will be a Greatest Hits album, set to be released for Christmas 2004. No immediate plans for his next album after that have been released yet, but it is guaranteed to cause a great furore as it will be his first without his songwriting partner Guy Chambers. Williams has, without doubt, proved himself as a singer and songwriter but there are still some critics that believe he relied a lot on Chambers' musical talent as a producer, to put the magic touches on the finished product – to make his singles into hits. Then again, towards the end of their collaboration, there was some criticism of *Escapology* being just a bit too polished. Some critics said it was produced so professionally that it meant that the vocals lost some of their raw edge.

Williams should never be underestimated, however. As he showed with *Swing When You're Winning*, he still has the ability to surprise, and make those surprises work to his advantage. He has the Midas touch and he's still got lots more to prove before, or if, if ever loses his crown.

ROBBIE WILLIAMS

DISCOGRAPHY

ALBUMS

Life Thru' a Lens (October 1997)
Highest chart position: 1
I've Been Expecting You (November 1998)
Highest chart position: 1
The Ego Has Landed (US release, 1999)
Sing When You're Winning (September 2000)
Highest chart position: 1
Swing When You're Winning (December 2001)
Highest chart position: 1
Escapology (November 2002)
Highest chart position: 1
Live At Knebworth (October 2003)
Highest chart position: 2

SINGLES

Freedom 96 (August 1996)
Highest chart position: 2
Old Before I Die (April 1997)
Highest chart position: 2
Lazy Days (July 1997)
Highest chart position: 8
South Of The Border   (September 1997)
Highest chart position: 14

ROBBIE WILLIAMS

DISCOGRAPHY

Angels (December 1997)
Highest chart position: 4
Let Me Entertain You (March 1998)
Highest chart position: 3
Millennium (September 1998)
Highest chart position: 1
No Regrets/Antmusic (December 1998)
Highest chart position: 4
Strong (March 1999)
Highest chart position: 4
She's The One/It's Only Us (November 1999)
Highest chart position: 1
Rock DJ (August 2000)
Highest chart position: 1
Kids (with Kylie Minogue) (October 2000)
Highest chart position: 2
Supreme (December 2000)
Highest chart position: 4
Let Love Be Your Energy (April 2001)
Highest chart position: 10
Eternity (July 2001)
Highest chart position: 1
Somethin´ Stupid (with Nicole Kidman) (Dec 2001)
Highest chart position: 1
Feel (December 2002)
Highest chart position: 2

ROBBIE WILLIAMS

DISCOGRAPHY

Come Undone (April 2003)
Highest chart position: 4
Something Beautiful (August 2003)
Highest chart position: 3
Sexed Up (November 2003)
Highest chart position: 10

OTHERS

Williams has also sung on the following albums:

20th Century Blues – Various Artists (Sept 1999)
Song – *...Bad Times Just Around The Corner*
Reload – Tom Jones (Sept 1999)
Song – *Are You Gonna Go My Way*
The Further Adventures – Jane Horrocks (Oct 2000)
Song – *That Old Black Magic*
Brand New Boots & Panties – Various (April
2001)
Song – *Sweet Gene Vincent*
Bridget Jones Diary –
Various/soundtrack (April 2001)
Song – *Have You Met Miss Jones?*
Song – *Not Of This Earth*
A Knight´s Tale – Various/soundtrack (June 2001)
Song – *We Are The Champions*

ROBBIE WILLIAMS

DISCOGRAPHY

Mike Bassett, England Manager –
Various/film soundtrack (Oct 2001)
Song – *Summertime*
Auntie Aubrey´s Excursions Vol. 2 – The Orb
(March 2002)
Song – *I Started A Joke* (feat. The Orb)
*Ten More Turntip*s – Ian Dury & The Blockheads
(March 2002)
Song – You're The Why
One Giant Leap (April 2002)
Song: My Culture
Johnny English (April 2003)
Song – *A Man For All Seasons*
Finding Nemo – Various/soundtrack (Nov 2003)
Song: *Beyond The Sea*

ROBBIE WILLIAMS

AWARDS

1998

European Music Awards – Best Male Solo Artist

GQ Magazine – Solo Artist of the Year

1999

Brit awards for Best Male Solo Artist, Best Single
– *Angels*, Best Video – *Millennium*

Ivor Novello Awards – Most Performed Song –
Angels; Songwriter of the Year (Robbie Williams
and Guy Chambers)

2000

Brit Awards for Best British Single – *She's The
One*; Best British Video – *She's The One*

Ivor Novello Awards:

Best Song lyrically & musically – *Strong* (Robbie
Williams and Guy Chambers)

European Music Award for Best Song – *Rock DJ*

Q Awards – Best Songwriter

Capital Radio Awards – Best Male Solo Artist,
Best British Single – *She's The One*

Best British Video – *She's The One*

My VH1 Music Award for Best UK Act

ROBBIE WILLIAMS

AWARDS

2001

Brit awards for Best Male Solo Artist, Best
British Single – *Rock DJ*; Best British Video –
Rock DJ
European Music Award – Best Male
MTV Video Music Award – Best Special Effects
In A Video – *Rock DJ*
MTV Europe Award – Best Male Act
GQ Magazine – Solo Artist of the year
Capital Radio Awards – Best Album – *Sing When
You're Winning*

2002

Brit award for Best Male Solo Artist
ECHO Award: Best International Male Artist

2003

Brit award for Best Male Solo Artist
World Music Award for Best British Pop/Rock
Male Artist
Q Award – Best Live Act

BIOGRAPHIES

OTHER BOOKS IN THE SERIES

Also available in the series:

Jennifer Aniston

David Beckham

George Clooney

Billy Connolly

Robert De Niro

Michael Douglas

Hugh Grant

Michael Jackson

Nicole Kidman

Jennifer Lopez

Madonna

Brad Pitt

Shane Richie

Jonny Wilkinson

OTHER BOOKS IN THE SERIES

JENNIFER ANISTON

She's been a Friend to countless millions worldwide, and overcame numerous hurdles to rise to the very top of her field. From a shy girl with a dream of being a famous actress, through being reduced to painting scenery for high school plays, appearing in a series of flop TV shows and one rather bad movie, Jennifer Aniston has persevered, finally finding success at the very top of the TV tree.

Bringing the same determination that got her a part on the world's best-loved TV series to her attempts at a film career, she's also worked her way from rom-com cutie up to serious, respected actress and box office draw, intelligently combining indie, cult and comedy movies into a blossoming career which looks set to shoot her to the heights of Hollywood's A-list. She's also found love with one of the world's most desirable men. Is Jennifer Aniston the ultimate Hollywood Renaissance woman? It would seem she's got more than a shot at such a title, as indeed, she seems to have it all, even if things weren't always that way. Learn all about Aniston's rise to fame in this compelling biography.

OTHER BOOKS IN THE SERIES

DAVID BECKHAM

This book covers the amazing life of the boy from East London who has not only become a world class footballer and the captain of England, but also an idol to millions, and probably the most famous man in Britain.

His biography tracks his journey, from the playing fields of Chingford to the Bernabau. It examines how he joined his beloved Manchester United and became part of a golden generation of talent that led to United winning trophies galore.

Beckham's parallel personal life is also examined, as he moved from tongue-tied football-obsessed kid to suitor of a Spice Girl, to one half of Posh & Becks, the most famous celebrity couple in Britain – perhaps the world. His non-footballing activities, his personal indulgences and changing styles have invited criticism, and even abuse, but his football talent has confounded the critics, again and again.

The biography looks at his rise to fame and his relationship with Posh, as well as his decision to leave Manchester for Madrid. Has it affected his relationship with Posh? What will the latest controversy over his sex life mean for celebrity's royal couple? And will he come back to play in England again?

OTHER BOOKS IN THE SERIES

GEORGE CLOONEY

The tale of George Clooney's astonishing career is an epic every bit as riveting as one of his blockbuster movies. It's a story of tenacity and determination, of fame and infamy, a story of succeeding on your own terms regardless of the risks. It's also a story of emergency rooms, batsuits, tidal waves and killer tomatoes, but let's not get ahead of ourselves.

Born into a family that, by Sixties' Kentucky standards, was dripping with show business glamour, George grew up seeing the hard work and heartache that accompanied a life in the media spotlight.

By the time stardom came knocking for George Clooney, it found a level-headed and mature actor ready and willing to embrace the limelight, while still indulging a lifelong love of partying and practical jokes. A staunchly loyal friend and son, a bachelor with a taste for the high life, a vocal activist for the things he believes and a born and bred gentleman; through failed sitcoms and blockbuster disasters, through artistic credibility and box office success, George Clooney has remained all of these things...and much, much more. Prepare to meet Hollywood's most fascinating megastar in this riveting biography.

OTHER BOOKS IN THE SERIES

BILLY CONNOLLY

In a 2003 London Comedy Poll to find Britain's favourite comedian, Billy Connolly came out on top. It's more than just Billy Connolly's all-round comic genius that puts him head and shoulders above the rest. Connolly has also proved himself to be an accomplished actor with dozens of small- and big-screen chalk marks to his name. In 2003, he could be seen in *The Last Samurai* with Tom Cruise.

Connolly has also cut the mustard in the USA, 'breaking' that market in a way that chart-topping pop groups since The Beatles and the Stones have invariably failed to do, let alone mere stand-up comedians. Of course, like The Beatles and the Stones, Billy Connolly has been to the top of the pop charts too with D.I.V.O.R.C.E. in 1975.

On the way he's experienced heartache of his own with a difficult childhood and a divorce of his own, found the time and energy to bring up five children, been hounded by the press on more than one occasion, and faced up to some considerable inner demons. But Billy Connolly is a survivor. Now in his 60s, he's been in show business for all of 40 years, and 2004 finds him still touring. This exciting biography tells the story an extraordinary entertainer.

OTHER BOOKS IN THE SERIES

ROBERT DE NIRO

Robert De Niro is cinema's greatest chameleon. Snarling one minute, smirking the next, he's straddled Hollywood for a quarter of a century, making his name as a serious character actor, in roles ranging from psychotic taxi drivers to hardened mobsters. The scowls and pent-up violence may have won De Niro early acclaim but, ingeniously, he's now playing them for laughs, poking fun at the tough guy image he so carefully cultivated. Ever the perfectionist, De Niro holds nothing back on screen, but in real life he is a very private man – he thinks of himself as just another guy doing a job. Some job, some guy. There's more to the man than just movies. De Niro helped New York pick itself up after the September 11 terrorist attacks on the Twin Towers by launching the TriBeCa Film Festival and inviting everyone downtown. He runs several top-class restaurants and has dated some of the most beautiful women in the world, least of all supermodel Naomi Campbell. Now in his 60s, showered with awards and a living legend, De Niro's still got his foot on the pedal. There are six, yes six, films coming your way in 2004. In this latest biography, you'll discover all about his latest roles and the life of this extraordinary man.

OTHER BOOKS IN THE SERIES

MICHAEL DOUGLAS

Douglas may have been a shaggy-haired member of a hippy commune in the Sixties but just like all the best laidback, free-loving beatniks, he's gone on to blaze a formidable career, in both acting and producing.

In a career that has spanned nearly 40 years so far, Douglas has produced a multitude of hit movies including the classic *One Flew Over The Cuckoo's Nest* and *The China Syndrome* through to box office smashes such as *Starman* and *Face/Off*.

His acting career has been equally successful – from *Romancing The Stone* to *Wall Street* to *Fatal Attraction*, Douglas's roles have shown that he isn't afraid of putting himself on the line when up there on the big screen.

His relationship with his father; his stay in a top clinic to combat his drinking problem; the breakdown of his first marriage; and his publicised clash with the British media have all compounded to create the image of a man who's transformed himself from being the son of Hollywood legend Kirk Douglas, into Kirk Douglas being the dad of Hollywood legend, Michael Douglas.

OTHER BOOKS IN THE SERIES

HUGH GRANT

He's the Oxford fellow who stumbled into acting, the middle-class son of a carpet salesman who became famous for bumbling around stately homes and posh weddings. The megastar actor who claims he doesn't like acting, but has appeared in over 40 movies and TV shows.

On screen he's romanced a glittering array of Hollywood's hottest actresses, and tackled medical conspiracies and the mafia. Off screen he's hogged the headlines with his high profile girlfriend as well as finding lifelong notoriety after a little Divine intervention in Los Angeles.

Hugh Grant is Britain's biggest movie star, an actor whose talent for comedy has often been misjudged by those who assume he simply plays himself.

From bit parts in Nottingham theatre, through comedy revues at the Edinburgh Fringe, and on to the top of the box office charts, Hugh has remained constant – charming, witty and ever so slightly sarcastic, obsessed with perfection and performance while winking to his audience as if to say: "This is all awfully silly, isn't it?" Don't miss this riveting biography.

OTHER BOOKS IN THE SERIES

MICHAEL JACKSON

Friday 29 August 1958 was not a special day in Gary, Indiana, and indeed Gary, was far from being a special place. But it was on this day and in this location that the world's greatest entertainer was to be born, Michael Joseph Jackson.

The impact that this boy was destined to have on the world of entertainment could never have been estimated. Here we celebrate Michael Jackson's extraordinary talents, and plot the defining events over his 40-year career. This biography explores the man behind the myth, and gives an understanding of what drives this special entertainer.

In 1993, there was an event that was to rock Jackson's world. His friendship with a 12-year-old boy and the subsequent allegations resulted in a lawsuit, a fall in record sales and a long road to recovery. Two marriages, three children and 10 years later there is a feeling of déjà vu as Jackson again deals with more controversy. Without doubt, 2004 proves to be the most important year in the singer's life. Whatever that future holds for Jackson, his past is secured, there has never been and there will never again be anything quite like Michael Jackson.

OTHER BOOKS IN THE SERIES

NICOLE KIDMAN

On 23 March 2003 Nicole Kidman won the Oscar for Best Actress for her role as Virginia Woolf in The Hours. That was the night that marked Nicole Kidman's acceptance into the upper echelons of Hollywood royalty. She had certainly come a long way from the 'girlfriend' roles she played when she first arrived in Hollywood – in films such as Billy Bathgate and Batman Forever – although even then she managed to inject her 'pretty girl' roles with an edge that made her acting stand out. And she was never merely content to be Mrs Cruise, movie star's wife. Although she stood dutifully behind her then husband in 1993 when he was given his star on the Hollywood Walk of Fame, Nicole got a star of her own 10 years later, in 2003.

Not only does Nicole Kidman have stunning good looks and great pulling power at the box office, she also has artistic credibility. But Nicole has earned the respect of her colleagues, working hard and turning in moving performances from a very early age. Although she dropped out of school at 16, no one doubts the intelligence and passion that are behind the fiery redhead's acting career, which includes television and stage work, as well as films. Find out how Kidman became one of Hollywood's most respected actresses in this compelling biography.

OTHER BOOKS IN THE SERIES

JENNIFER LOPEZ

There was no suggestion that the Jennifer Lopez of the early Nineties would become the accomplished actress, singer and icon that she is today. Back then she was a dancer on the popular comedy show In Living Color – one of the Fly Girls, the accompaniment, not the main event. In the early days she truly was Jenny from the block; the Bronx native of Puerto Rican descent – another hopeful from the east coast pursuing her dreams in the west.

Today, with two marriages under her belt, three multi-platinum selling albums behind her and an Oscar-winning hunk as one of her ex-boyfriends, she is one of the most talked about celebrities of the day. Jennifer Lopez is one of the most celebrated Hispanic actresses of all time.

Her beauty, body and famous behind, are lusted after by men and envied by women throughout the world. She has proven that she can sing, dance and act. Yet her critics dismiss her as a diva without talent. And the criticisms are not just about her work, some of them are personal. But what is the reality? Who is Jennifer Lopez, where did she come from and how did get to where she is now? This biography aims to separate fact from fiction to reveal the real Jennifer Lopez.

OTHER BOOKS IN THE SERIES

MADONNA

Everyone thought they had Madonna figured out in early 2003. The former Material Girl had become Maternal Girl, giving up on causing controversy to look after her two children and set up home in England with husband Guy Ritchie. The former wild child had settled down and become respectable. The new Madonna would not do anything to shock the establishment anymore, she'd never do something like snogging both Britney Spears and Christina Aguilera at the MTV Video Music Awards... or would she?

Of course she would. Madonna has been constantly reinventing herself since she was a child, and her ability to shock even those who think they know better is both a tribute to her business skills and the reason behind her staying power. Only Madonna could create gossip with two of the current crop of pop princesses in August and then launch a children's book in September. In fact, only Madonna would even try.

In her 20-year career she has not just been a successful pop singer, she is also a movie star, a business woman, a stage actress, an author and a mother. Find out all about this extraordinary modern-day icon in this new compelling biography.

OTHER BOOKS IN THE SERIES

BRAD PITT

From the launch pad that was his scene stealing turn in *Thelma And Louise* as the sexual-enlightening bad boy. To his character-driven performances in dramas such as *Legends of the Fall* through to his Oscar-nominated work in *Twelve Monkeys* and the dark and razor-edged Tyler Durden in *Fight Club*, Pitt has never rested on his laurels. Or his good looks.

And the fact that his love life has garnered headlines all over the world hasn't hindered Brad Pitt's profile away from the screen either – linked by the press to many women, his relationships with the likes of Juliette Lewis and Gwyneth Paltrow. Then of course, in 2000, we had the Hollywood fairytale ending when he tied the silk knot with Jennifer Aniston.

Pitt's impressive track record as a superstar, sex symbol *and* credible actor looks set to continue as he has three films lined up for release over the next year – as Achilles in the Wolfgang Peterson-helmed Troy; Rusty Ryan in the sequel *Ocean's Twelve* and the titular Mr Smith in the thriller *Mr & Mrs Smith* alongside Angelina Jolie. Pitt's ever-growing success shows no signs of abating. Discover all about Pitt's meteoric rise from rags to riches in this riveting biography.

OTHER BOOKS IN THE SERIES

SHANE RICHIE

Few would begrudge the current success of 40-year-old Shane Richie. To get where he is today, Shane has had a rather bumpy roller coaster ride that has seen the hard working son of poor Irish immigrants endure more than his fair share of highs and lows – financially, professionally and personally.

In the space of four decades he has amused audiences at school plays, realised his childhood dream of becoming a Pontins holiday camp entertainer, experienced homelessness, beat his battle with drink, became a million-aire then lost the lot. He's worked hard and played hard.

When the producers of *EastEnders* auditioned Shane for a role in the top TV soap, they decided not to give him the part, but to create a new character especially for him. That character was Alfie Moon, manager of the Queen Vic pub, and very quickly Shane's TV alter ego has become one of the most popular soap characters in Britain. This biography is the story of a boy who had big dreams and never gave up on turning those dreams into reality.

OTHER BOOKS IN THE SERIES

JOHNNY WILKINSON

"There's 35 seconds to go, this is the one. It's coming back for Jonny Wilkinson. He drops for World Cup glory. It's over! He's done it! Jonny Wilkinson is England's Hero yet again..."

That memorable winning drop kick united the nation, and lead to the start of unprecedented victory celebrations throughout the land. In the split seconds it took for the ball to leave his boot and slip through the posts, Wilkinson's life was to change forever. It wasn't until three days later, when the squad flew back to Heathrow and were met with a rapturous reception, that the enormity of their win, began to sink in.

Like most overnight success stories, Wilkinson's journey has been a long and dedicated one. He spent 16 years 'in rehearsal' before achieving his finest performance, in front of a global audience of 22 million, on that rainy evening in Telstra Stadium, Sydney.

But how did this modest self-effacing 24-year-old become England's new number one son? This biography follows Jonny's journey to international stardom. Find out how he caught the rugby bug, what and who his earliest influences were and what the future holds for our latest English sporting hero.